# Annuals

# Cullen Garden Guide

# Annuals

## by Mark Cullen

**Summerhill Press Ltd.**
**Toronto**

© Mark Cullen

Published by Summerhill Press Ltd
Published by Toronto, Ontario

Cover Photography: Dieter Hessel

Editor : Judith Drynan
Illustrations: Lynn McIlvride Evans

**Canadian Cataloguing in Publication Data**

Cullen, Mark, 1956-
  Annuals

(Cullen Canadian garden guide)
ISBN 0-920197-24-8

1. Annuals (Plants) — Canada.   2. Flower gardening.
I. Title.   II. Series.

SB422.C84 1986     635.9'312    C86-093011-4


Distributed in Canada by:
Collier Macmillan Canada
50 Gervais Drive
Don Mills, Ontario M3C 3K4

Printed and Bound in Canada

To Howard Bunston, who will never stop working and sharing his great garden.

# Contents

# Letter From Mark

Nature is wonderful. Every year our barren winter landscape comes miraculously alive in the warmth of spring, and plants and flowers start to grow once more. For me, one of the things which enhances the joy of this renewal is a garden full of colourful, fast-growing annuals.

Annuals are flowers or foliage plants which complete their entire life cycle in one season. This means that they have to be planted every year, but the pleasure they bring is always worth the effort. These happy, healthy plants provide a profusion of blooms for a minimum of time, effort and money, and their great variety means that you should have no difficult finding the best flowers for your particular garden — whether it is a container or a large border.

Although the growing period is usually only five or six months, you can always find plenty to do with your annual garden. In the winter, when you're not planting or tending the flowers, you can be planning things for the coming summer — looking at catalogues and drawing up lists. Then when spring comes, you can celebrate the arrival of longer and warmer days by getting your hands into the earth, sitting back on your heels every once in a while to survey your work. There is nothing quite like watching the rapid growth of an annual border, with the tiniest seeds becoming tall graceful plants in what seems like no time at all.

In this book I tried to give you all the information necessary to make gardening a happy experience, without overloading you with too much or confusing you with too little. There are detailed descriptions of thirty-five of the most popular annuals in the country, plus a handy chart.

I have also given you instructions for making a Super Composter to use up your kitchen scraps, tips on how to choose the best flowers for specialty gardens, and a selection of necessary tools and materials.

8

Annuals give us variety from year to year and are especially useful for those of us who must move from place to place and into houses with no existing gardens. Many of our most popular annuals originated in the wilderness of tropical zones. Now, by planting them in our gardens every summer, we can bring some of that colour and lush beauty right into our own backyards.

Happy Gardening,

**Mark Cullen**

# Chapter One

## Tools

The tools for planting and taking care of annuals are so simple and basic that similar ones were probably used thousands of years ago by the first cultivators. They are all hand tools and unmechanized, so that unless your neighbour is using a power mower to cut the lawn, you can enjoy the peace and quiet of working in the earth — one of the chief joys of gardening.

### How To Buy Tools

If you are just starting out in the gardening game, you may be tempted to buy inexpensive tools. You should resist this temptation strenuously. Here's why. Cheap tools break, rust and rot, and then you have to replace them. There is no saving in this, particularly when you consider that it might cost you even more to replace them than it did to buy them in the first place.

On the other hand, good quality tools last longer and function better. So you win on two counts. Get ones of tempered steel, and forged rather than stamped. You don't necessarily have to buy them new, either.

Look for contents sales where people are moving out of their house into an apartment or condominium. These sales can often provide good gardening equipment at a fraction of the cost. You can clean off any rust with inexpensive rust remover, and either sharpen the tools yourself or take them to the hardware store and have it done for you.

### Care Of Tools

If you buy tools with wooden handles, either new or second-hand, give them a couple of coats of oil-based paint or spray. This will not only make them easy to locate in the garden, but protect them

*The trowel is the tool you'll use most to dig holes for bedding plants, so buy a good one.*

against the elements just in case you forget and leave them out in the rain.

It is a good idea to have a place to store your tools — easy to get to and close to the garden. A shed is ideal, but a garage is also good. Save space by hanging them on the wall between specially placed nails or pegs. A good way to keep them clean is to place a bucket of sand with oil mixed into it close to the storage area. Just before you put your tools away, dunk them in and out of the oily sand. This will clean off any dirt, and prevent the tools from getting rusty.

## Basic And Necessary

*Trowel.* This is the tool you will be using constantly to dig small holes and mix in amendments when setting out bedding plants. In fact, trowels are so important that it is a good idea to have two or more. Be sure to buy ones which are heavy to the heft, yet comfortable when you grip the handle. They should be smooth and strong where the steel joins the handle. If this joint is composed of two pieces welded together, it will probably weaken and break with use.

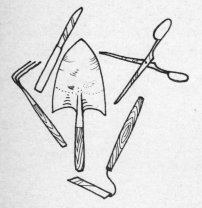

*Hand tools are necessary for annual planting and maintenance — especially for flowers in containers and raised gardens.*

*Cultivators.* The three curved prongs in these tools are wonderful for bresaking up the earth. The small hand cultivator is useful for loosening the soil around plants during the growing season without damaging the roots. It is particularly good for low-growing plants and raised gardens. The large one is excellent for the areas between rows and around large sturdy plants.

*Knife.* You should have at least one knife with a rounded tip and sharp, smooth blade. It will be useful for cutting out bedding plants from flats, and digging out errant weeds. Carry it with you as you do your gardening. You'll be surprised how often you use it.

*Scissors.* With annuals, this is the only pruning tool you'll need. Get ones with blunt ends so you can carry them around in your back pocket without fear of a nasty sharp surprise. Use them to cut off dead or weak side branches, as well as the fading blooms on tough-stemmed plants like geraniums. Of course, you will also want to use them to gather fresh flowers for the house — especially from those plants which need to be cut every day or two to keep blooming.

*Hoes.* Some people think hoes are rather old-fashioned. I think they are indispensable. The small hand hoes can clear the weeds away from tender seedlings, and are good for cleaning up the earth in raised gardens as

*A small hoe is helpful for keeping weeds away from young seedlings.*

well. The large hoe is still the best tool for going down between the rows of a picking garden to remove any weeds and grass. Keep the blades good and sharp and make sure the hoes are made of forged steel.

*Fork.* Here is a handy tool. Use it to turn the earth in the early spring and to break up large clumps. When you start to prepare the soil for planting, the fork is excellent for mixing in amendments like peat moss, compost and manure.

It is also handy for forking the compost out of the bin and into the wheelbarrow, and for lifting up piles of straw or cut grass. Use it to lift and spread heavy mulch material like leaf mold and straw.

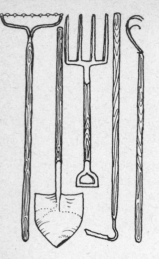

*Large tools — cultivator, hoe, fork, spade and rake — are essential for soil preparation and maintenance.*

*Shovel or Spade.* The most practical kind for annual gardening is the basic D-handled pointed spade — for digging down and turning hard soil in the early spring, applying peat moss and mulch, and carving out new garden beds.

*Rake.* There is nothing better for smoothing out the earth and making it finely textured. This is particularly important when you are going to be planting seeds. The light sprinkling of soil covering the planted seeds can then be tamped down by the bottom of the rake's tines.

*Whellbarrow.* The wheelbarrow is still the best thing for transporting tools, mulch, compost, peat moss, plants and anything else that wants to get from one place to another in the garden. It also provides a good mixing area for amendments like peat moss and manure before putting them in the planting holes. There are many models available, some with two tires, and some with one pneumatic tire. Plastic wheelbarrows are lighter and won't rust, but if you are going to be doing heavy work like building a rock garden, a steel one would be better. To prevent rust, paint it with a non-toxic oil-based paint before using.

*Hose.* Get a hose which is 3/4″ in diameter because it carries more water than thinner ones. A rubberized plastic hose is good because it will stay flexible and won't cramp up even in cool weather.

*Water Nozzles.* You must water seedlings and young bedding plants very gently. Attach a sprayer on the end of the hose which will give a fine mist. For grown plants, one of the best things you can invest in is a soaker hose. This lies on the ground right beside the plants and the water comes out steady and low. The soaker hose gives you three big advantages. The mulch and earth get an even amount of water, the leaves don't get wet (causing mildew and spotting in some plants), and the flower heads don't get heavy with water and break off.

*Bug Sprayers.* Annuals have very few problems with bugs, and those that show up can usually be dealt with by using a powder or an aerosol spray. But sometimes larger areas may have problems which call for stronger measures. In this case you can buy a cannister with a pump spray, or attach the inexpensive and easy to use Dial-A-Spray® to the end of your hose.

**Miscellaneous**
- Garden gloves.
- Bucket to mix water-soluble fertilizer.
- A piece of foam or rubber to kneel on.
- A soil tester to test the pH of the earth.
- Black string to keep the birds away.
- Green bamboo stakes the support tall annuals.
- Tomato cages to support airy plants like cosmos.

# Chapter Two

## Materials

There are three materials necessary for the successful growing of most annuals — soil amendments, mulch and fertilizers.

### Soil Amendments

The majority of annuals like soil which is light, crumbly and well-draining. Unfortunately, not all soil is like this, and so the gardener has to amend or improve it every spring with organic material.

*Peat Moss.* This is the material from bogs or marshes which is partially composted and then dried, and is one of the best soil amendments you can buy. I would never start planting a garden without it. When added to the soil it makes it friable (a term used in gardening which means light and crumbly), and also helps to hold the moisture long enough to give the plants a drink.

At the same time, it allows the water to drain away quickly so that the air can continue to

*Three of the best ingredients for enriching the soil are peat moss, manure and compost.*

more fun and ecologically sensible to make your own. Compost is simply plant and vegetable matter which has broken down into crumbly tilth. When added to any soil, it acts the same way as peat moss, and also adds valuable nourishing ingredients. Underneath every good garden you will usually find compost. move about in the earth and give the roots the oxygen they need for the plant's health. Make sure that when you put peat moss in the soil you also moisten it. That way it doesn't steal moisture from the surrounding earth.

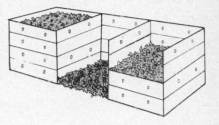

*The three-bin composter is a classic. You not only get wonderful soil enrichment from the compost, but make efficient use of vegetable scraps and garden cuttings as well.*

*Manure.* This is one of the oldest and most effective ways of enriching the soil. One of its drawbacks has been that it not only encouraged the growth of plants, but the growth of weed seeds as well — seeds which came in the manure itself. It is now possible to buy manure at the nursery which has been sterilized and is weed-free. Sheep and cattle manure are equally good for plants that like fertile soil and the rich life.

*Compost.* You can buy composted material from the nursery, but it is less expensive,

## The Compost Bin

I have described in detail how to build a three-part compost bin in my book "Vegetables and Bush Fruits." Basically the idea is this. Build the bins from plywood, with slats on the side to allow the air in. (Oxygen is needed to help break down the material and reduce odour.) Then put in all your kitchen scraps, except meat and fats, and every six inches add a layer of grass cuttings, chopped leaves or peat moss. Add lots of crushed eggshells and some liquid fertilizer with a high nitogen content to help the material break down faster. When the pile in one bin gets almost to the top, fork it into the second bin, and start again with the first bin. When that is full, move everything over one bin. When the first bin is full again, use the completely composted material in the third bin in your garden.

## The Super Composter

The three-part compost method is fine if you have a fairly large property, but it isn't too practical for smaller gardens. For this reason, commercial plastic composters have become popular-ranging in price from $60 to $160. However, you can achieve the same results for far less money, by using the homemade Super Composter. This includes the best aerator and composter in nature — the common earthworm.

### What You'll Need

- Two large plastic garbage bins
- Earthworms
- Kitchen scraps except meat, bones and fat
- Crushed eggshells
- Grass cuttings or finely cut evergreen needles
- Earth, peat moss or manure

Get plastic garbage bins with turn-lock lids, preferably in a dark colour. Into one of them, put a layer of earth, peat moss, or manure, and then start filling with vegetable peelings and all kinds of kitchen scraps.

When the pile reaches about four inches, add another layer of peat moss (or grass and evergreen cuttings) and ... some earthworms. Look in the phone book for live bait places and garden centres which sell them.

Keep adding ingredients, including as many crushed egg shells as possible, and every once in a while lift the material up and aerate it with a gardening fork. Keep the lid on between additions. The earthworms will move through the material making the best humus in the world — they do all the work and get all the benefits. (It is no coincidence that the most successful commercial compost has a picture of an earthworm on the front of the bag.)

When the first bin is full, fork it into the second bin so the top material is now on the bottom. Cover and leave for several days — then, start all over again.

This sounds odd, but it makes compost quickly, even in the winter. Put the bins in a place where they will get the sun. and this heat along with the dart plastic, will keep the interior warm. Because the earthworms are aerating the material, it doesn't require vents or get smelly.

When you are ready to use the compost, fork it into the garden, along with the earthworms, to make your garden rich and productive.

## Mulch

This is what you put on the top of the earth around the plants. It keeps the moisture level of the soil constant and the roots cool, even in hot weather. It also keeps down the weeds. Mulch is the gardener's good helper. If you go to all the trouble and expense of planting a garden and don't put down any mulch, you aren't going to have the success you deserve. Although there are a number of different materials you can use, like black plastic sheeting, annuals usually call for something attractive as well as practical.

*Peat Moss.* This is somewhat effective. It will enrich the soil as it breaks down, but when allowed to dry out will repel water. Replace when necessary.

*Wood Chips.* Pine and cedar chips are very attractive, keep the weeds firmly under control, and smell good. They may seem expensive at first, but will outlast almost any other kind of mulch.

*Pebbles.* These don't break down or add any nutrients to the soil, but the white ones can be very attractive — especially in a raised garden with colourful plants like geraniums.

For places where the earth isn't so visible, one of the best mulches is leaf mold. Here is an inexpensive and easy way to get this excellent mulch. In the autumn, put your fallen and raked leaves into black plastic garbage bags. (If possible, shred the leaves first.)

Put the bags against a side wall which gets the sun during the winter, and the first hot rays in the spring. By the time you have set out your plants and seeds in late spring, the leaves will be pliable enough to be used as mulch.

Leaf mold will eventually break down so that in the fall you can fork it under and let it add nutrients to the soil for the next year.

## Fertilizers

All annuals perform best when a regular dose of fertilizer is applied. Manure worked into the soil before planting will give them a good beginning, as will a fertilizer like Plant Start — designed to encourage good and rapid root development.

The three numbers on the packages of fertilizer refer to nitrogen, phosphorous and potassium. Flowering annuals will be encouraged to bloom with the application of a high phosphorous fertilizer like 6-12-12. Spread 2 lb. per 100 sq. ft. before planting and one handful per plant each month after planting. Foliage plants like Coleus perform well when fed a balanced water soluable fertilizer.

# Chapter Three

## Planning The Garden

The wonderful thing about annuals is that you can plant new kinds of flowers every year and change the whole look of your garden. The not-so-wonderful thing about annuals is that every year you must make new decisions. The solution to this is easy. Make a plan on paper. Don't rely on the hit-and-miss method of gardening if you want the most for your time and money. Plan carefully. This is one of the most important steps toward creating beautiful surroundings and the one which is, unfortunately, most often ignored.

Draw a survey or plot plan of your lot and plant beds, and divide into sections for different flowers. Figure out how many plants you'll need to buy or sow by pacing the area off...making each pace equal about three feet.

Most annual plants should be set out at either two plants or one plant to a foot — depending on height and spread. If you have a very large bed in the sun,

you might want to consider direct seeding for a cutting garden.

The chart in this book, and the descriptions of thirty-five of the most popular and easy to grow annuals, will help you plan. Read the detailed descriptions carefully and decide what plants suit you, what plants go with other plants, and how many you'll need. Then make list. Take these lists to the nursery with you when you go to buy your plants, so you will have something to go on besides a fuzzy idea in your head. I've often seen people walking around looking at bedding plants with a dazed expression on their faces. They just don't have any idea what they want. Plan your garden taking into account four important things — light, soil, colour and height.

### Light

Light is very important tc

annuals. Since many of these plants are originally from warm, sunny, and sometimes tropical climates, they need a certain amount of sunlight to grow properly. These are the plants which have "full sun" written beside their names. However, many people are faced with the problem of an area in full or partial shade. These beds are more difficult to plan for, since sun-loving plants in shady areas will grow all spindly or not at all. Some will survive, but develop long stems and small flowers. Fortunately there are some very attractive annual flowers which perform well in shade or partial shade. Here are the shade-loving plants discussed later in the book in some detail.

| | |
|---|---|
| Impatiens | Dusty Millar |
| Wax Begonia | Lobelia |
| Browallia | Nicotiana |
| Ageratum | Pansy |
| Coleus | Viola |
| Salvia | |

## Soil

Good soil is a treasure for the gardener. To test your own soil, take a handful and squeeze it ... then open your hand. If it stays together in a ball and then crumbles, you've got loam ... the best kind of soil. If it remains in a firm ball without crumbling, it's got too much clay in it, and if it falls all over the place when you poke it, you have sandy soil.

Some annuals, like calendula, portulaca and gazania, grow well in sandy soil, and others like nasturtiums, thrive in average to poor soil.

Clay soil must be amended, however, before anything can survive in it. When the sun hits it, the surface gets hard, water can't soak in, and eventually the plants just choke up and die.

There are a number of plants which like alkaline soil. If you don't have it naturally, you can create it by adding lime. When you are planning your garden, you might want to have one bed planted with these alkaline-loving flowers. Here are some of the plants in this book.

| | |
|---|---|
| Alyssum | Dianthus or |
| Baby's Breath | Pinks |
| Carnation | Sweet Pea |
| Cosmos | Sweet William |

## Colour

One of the most delightful aspects of annuals is the wide range of vivid colours they can add to our gardens. With a little planning, we can use that variety to good advantage. Look at the colour wheel and you will see the basic colours and how they relate to one another. Of course, this doesn't include all

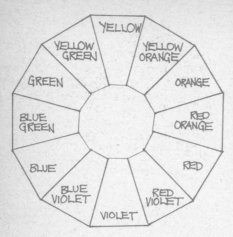

*The colour wheel can give you a good idea of which basic colours are compatible and which are complimentary.*

flaming salvia will certainly be noticed — even at a distance. Don't forget white in your choice of colours, but remember that white and silver really stand out especially when used as accents for the more vivid colours.

Consult the individual descriptions of plants and the chart in this book for colour ideas, and make a mental note of combinations you admire in other gardens or parks.

## Height

the shades, but it gives you some idea. Pick a colour. The colours on each side will be harmonious. The colour across and on each side will be dramatic and complimentary. For example, a bed of yellow marigolds will go well with other marigolds in orange and gold or, (looking across the chart) with violet alyssum, blue ageratum or red-violet petunias.

The chart divides the colour spectrum into the cool colours, greens and blues, and the warm colours, reds and yellows. Cool colours tend to be better close up — a bed of dark leafy ferns at the bottom of the garden will hardly be seen, whereas a bed of

When you're planning a border, you must be sure to get not only the type of flower you want, but also the variety which will grow to the right height. It only makes sense that tall plants will be at the back of the border, medium in the middle and low or ground-hugging plants at the front. However, if you are generally looking at your garden from the patio at the back of your house, you may want to try putting the tall flowers at the far end of the border, and plant the others down in height as the border comes toward your vision. Use your imagination and you will find plenty of other ways to use heights in the garden for visual pleasure.

## The Garden Journal

One of the ways to produce better and better gardens every year is to keep a journal. It doesn't have to be complicated. Put your drawings and plans in, and also photographs of your gardens as they looked in their prime. Make notes of which plants did well in which areas, and take special note of those that did poorly. Keep a record of plants which should be rotated season by season, like asters, and the places they have been planted. Tape in the seed packets your used, and write down the varieties and types of annuals which grew well together.

Keeping a garden journal is easy and can make every year's planting better and more creative.

## Different Gardens

Gardens can be more than a border along the side of the garden. You can create different kinds of flower gardens to enhance your property and your enjoyment. Plan each one out with the best plants for that particular spot, and use your imagination. I once drilled some holes in the bottom of an old portable barbecue, filled it with soil, and planted it with petunias. Then I just wheeled it around wherever I wanted and wherever the light was best. It was the hit of the season.

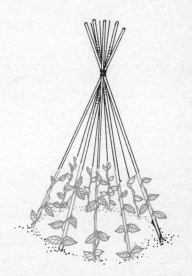

Annuals don't have to be planted just in borders against the house or fence. Grow sweet peas up a teepee for an interesting shape or to hide something.

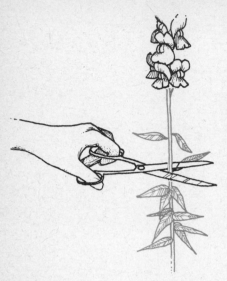

## Twilight Garden

If you sit outside in the evening, a twilight garden filled with beautifully scented flowers can be lovely. Experiment with different plants and choose ones with a luminous quality. Here are some to start with.

| | |
|---|---|
| Ageratum | Lobelia |
| Alyssum (White or purple) | White Impatiens |
| Dusty Miller | White Nicotiana |
| Heliotrope | |

## Cutting Garden

An old-fashioned cutting garden is practical and wonderful if you have room for it. This is exactly what it sounds like — a garden with flowers which are good for cutting. Traditionally, these flowers are tall, and planted in rows with space to walk between. (Set down boards so the earth doesn't get compacted.) Most annuals love to be picked as it encourages blooms, but there are some which actually need to be cut regularly if they are to continue to produce flowers. The asterisk marks these plants.

*While most annuals benefit from cutting, some actually need to be kept cut to continue blooming.*

## Patio Plants

These are plants which, because of their scent and appearance, are good around the patio in small beds and in containers. Some of the plants suitable for container gardening in this book are:

| | |
|---|---|
| Alyssum | Nicotiana |
| Gypsophila or Baby's Breath | Salvia |
| Canna Lily | Sweet Pea |
| Geranium | Thunbergia vine |
| Lobelia | Vinca |

| | |
|---|---|
| Gysophila or Baby's Breath | Nasturiums* |
| Carnation | Snapdragons* |
| Cosmos | Zinnias* |
| Dahlia | Dianthus or Pinks* |
| Marigolds | |

## Containers and Hanging Baskets

Flowers planted in containers need more attention than those set out in gardens, but the effect is often worth it. Use in classic locations like the patio and front verandah, and also in places where the flowers will surprise the eye. I sometimes like to hang small baskets filled with shade-loving impatients from the branches and trunks of trees.

## Raised Gardens

You can build raised gardens using rocks, concrete blocks, railway ties, or bricks — then fill the top 12 inches with amended soil. Raised gardens are becoming more and more popular. They not only add variety to the landscape, but eliminate many of the problems of inground beds. You can literally create your own soil using earth or commercial topsoil, manure, and peat moss or compost. You can place the garden exactly where you want it to get the right kind of light for the flowers you want to plant, and look after it more easily. Raised gardens can also be built near one another but at different heights to add interest and to please the eye. Plants, especially low growing plants, are set off to better advantage because they are higher off the ground.

*Try something a little different like planting containers with shade-loving impatiens and hanging from a tree branch.*

*Raised gardens are becoming more and more popular. They put the flowers where they can be seen, and give the gardener more control over soil conditions.*

*Use fast-climbing vines to hide unsightly objects such as garbage cans in the side walkway.*

## Special Uses

Annuals can also be used for special and practical purposes. You can plant vines like thunbergia and sweet pea to give you privacy, and to hide unsightly objects like garbage cans in the sideway. Make a teepee of stakes and let the vines grow up them. You can do this anywhere by digging a round trench and amending the soil with peat moss and composted cattle manure. The teepee can hide things like concrete topped wells.

Sand-loving plants like gazania and portulaca can be used in poor soil areas like driveway strips, or between the cracks in paving stones, so you get flowers instead of weeds and grass. Cascading petunias from window boxes can break the monotony of aluminum siding, and if you plant flowers like nasturtiums and marigolds, they will help keep away the bugs from their neighbours.

# Chapter Four

## Planting The Garden

Unless you want to grow your own seedlings indoors (see my chapter on propagation in "Houseplants"), the best way to grow annuals is either by direct seeding into the place where you want the flowers to grow, or by setting out bedding plants you buy at the nursery. First, however, you have to prepare the soil.

### In The Fall

Pull any dead or withered plants out of the garden. Then either throw them away, or cut them up and add to the compost heap. Turn the soil over with a spade, burying any weeds, grass, and mulch material which can decompose. These will add nutrients and tilth to the soil as they break down. You can cover the beds with a mulch like fallen leaves if you like. This will keep the soil warmer so it can be worked earlier in the spring. Some people like a mulch of straw, but I avoid it as it attracts mice.

### In The Spring

As soon as the soil can be worked in the early spring, go out and turn it over with a spade or fork ... whacking the big clumps out. This will give the soil a chance to warm up as the sun starts to shine longer and hotter. Don't be fooled as the days get warmer, though. Most annuals only get a good start in life if they are planted in warm soil. Sometimes it's a great temptation to start planting on those hot May days, but you should always remember that it is the temperature of the *soil* which is important to young plants — not the temperature of the air.

A good way to test the earth to see if it is warm enough to cultivate and plant is to take a handful and squeeze it — then hold it for a minute. If it feels cool, or if your hand is clammy when you put the earth back, you shouldn't plant in it. Wait until the soil is warm to the touch.

## Preparing The Soil

**What You'll Need:**
- Spade
- Gardening fork
- Earthworms (optional)
- Peat moss
- Composted Cattle Manure
- Lime
- Garden Compost (optional)
- Rake

This is the important part — when you prepare the soil specifically for the flowers you want to grow. Turn the earth one more time with the fork, until all the clumps are out and the soil is in small particles. Then add the amendments you need — usually peat moss and/or compost. Some lime will make the soil alkaline. Now, smooth out with a rake.
(Don't forget to add nature's best natural composters, earthworms. Buy them from live bait store or gardening centres.) For convenience, you can amend individual holes for bedding plants.

## Amending The Soil

Most annuals, although not all of them, like soil which is average to rich, and which drains well. Since most areas don't

*To save time and money when setting out bedding plants, amend only the holes where the plants will grow. Add peat moss or compost and mix with the earth.*

have such perfect soil, our garden earth must be fixed or amended every year before planting. Put two inches of organic material — either peat moss, compost, manure, or a mixture — on the earth. Then mix it into the top six or eight inches. The final mix should be at least one third organic matter, so don't skimp. You'll only suffer disappointment later when your flowers aren't doing as well as they should. Adding organic materials has a number of advantages.
1. The soil will be more friable (light and crumbly) so oxygen can get in, and the roots can spread out.

2. Organic material gives the plants a continuous supply of necessary nutrients.
3. It allows the soil to hold water long enough to give the plants a drink, and then lets the moisture drain away so the roots can get oxygen.

Check the individual charts of annuals in this book to find out what plants are particularly fond of lightly to highly amended soil.

## Acid and Alkaline Soils

Most annuals like soil on the acid side with the pH measuring about 6.5. Some, like the geranium, even like a drink of acid every once in a while in the form of diluted apple cider vinegar. But there are a number of excellent border and cutting flowers which grow well in alkaline soil with the pH at about 7.5. This is where your pH soil tester comes in. This inexpensive and easy-to-use kit is available at gardening centres and will tell you what your soil's pH level is.

Peat moss will bring the pH down and make it more acid, and lime will make it more alkaline. Sprinkle lime on cultivated soil until it forms a white film, then squiggle it into the top six inches with a gardening fork. You can test again, but this will usually give you good alkaline conditions.

## Before Planting

Once your soil is cultivated, rake it fine and transfer the plans you made on paper onto the earth. Trace the sections out with the end of the rake and put the seed packages and boxes of bedding plants in the sections you want them to grow in just to see what the finished project will look like. Believe it or not, this works, and helps make the grown garden better.

## Sowing Seeds

If you are planting large seeds, like nasturtiums and sweet

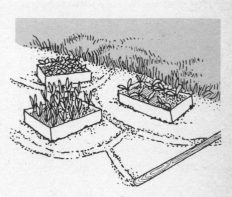

*When the soil is ready for planting, convert your garden designs from paper onto the earth with the end of your rake. Then you can see the sections and what will go in them.*

peas, you can just poke them into the prepared earth the appropriate distance apart. Smaller seeds are a little more difficult to sow. Here's a trick to make it easier. Put some sand into a shallow bowl and mix in the fine seeds. Then broadcast this mixture widely over a well-raked cultivated area, and tamp down with a fine layer of soil. The sand will prevent the seeds from falling too close together and the flowers from growing in clumps.

*Mix small seeds with sand so you can sow them more evenly.*

## Mixed Annuals

Sometimes it's fun, especially for children, to plant a variety seed pack like Mixed Annuals. I once did this in a sunny front border and got a wonderful display of riotous colour which lasted all summer. Although there was very little work involved, it was interesting to water the seedlings and wonder what was coming up. You can make your own mixed annuals by following the charts and buying individual seed packets, then mixing the different seeds together. Here is a list of the annuals in this book which are best planted out as seeds into the area where the flowers will grow.

| | |
|---|---|
| Alyssum | Ornamental Grasses |
| Aster | Marigold |
| Baby's Breath | Morning Glory |
| Calendula | Nasturtium |
| Cosmos | Portulaca |
| Gazania | Sweet Pea |
| | Zinnia |

## Bedding Plants

The best bedding plants should be fresh-looking and squat — never leggy. They should not be in flower when you plant them, and ideally, they should not even be in bud. However, most garden centers provide annuals in bloom because that is what most people want. Know what varieties you want before you

Buy young bedding plants which are squat — not leggy — and fresh-looking.

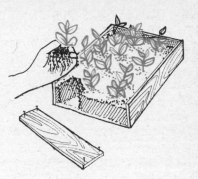

Depending on how strongly the roots have grown together in flats, you can either tear the plants apart. . . . .

go to the nursery, so you can be sure of the colours without actually seeing them on the young plants. Don't buy bedding plants with a lot of roots coming out of the bottom of the container.

## How To Plant

Bedding plants can come in flats, either one with all the plants growing together, or one with individual containers. As soon as you get them home the nursery, put the flats in a place which gets filtered sunlight, and keep the soil moist until ready to set out.

There are two ways of getting the plants out of flats where they are all growing together and the roots are tangled up. You can pull smaller plants apart, but you must do this very

. . . .or cut them with a knife or trowel.

gently so that the roots will suffer the least amount of trauma possible. You may have to cut stronger plants apart with a knife or the edge of a trowel. Fortunately, these bedding plants (like marigolds) are usually sturdy enough to stand up to this kind of treatment.

The best time to set out bedding plants is when the soil is warm and the sun is in. Dig a hole just big enough for the plant to fit into and deep enough so that when the young plant is put into the hole, the earth lines will be the same. You might want to put a handful of peat moss into the filling-in earth to help the plant get started. After the hole is filled in, tamp down the earth with your hands. That's all there is to to it.

*Use a fine-spray nozzle on your hose to water young seeds, plants and seedlings.*

## Watering

Make sure seedlings and bedding plants aren't overcome by strong jets of water from the hose. Use an attachment with a fine spray and keep the soil damp but not soaked.

## Fertilizing

Add a mild solution of a fertilizer like Plant Start® when you set your new plants out. This will reduce the shock of transplant and help in root development.

# Chapter Five

## Plant Care

Once your seeds or bedding plants are in the earth, they must be cared for gently until they are responsible adults.

As seeds sprout and become seedlings, it will be necessary to thin them. Since the roots may be growing together with the roots of other seedlings under the ground, the best way to do this is to cut them out at soil level with a pair of scissors. It may seem cruel to cut away perfectly good seedlings, but remember that some must fall for the good of those which will grow ahead — particularly if the fallen ones are put on the compost heap.

Keep the weeds down by gently hoeing with a small hoe, and as soon as the plants are big enough not to be smothered, lay some good mulch material around them, such as Canada Red Bark Mulch.

Some plants, like marigolds, will grow much bushier if you pinch out the growing tips as they develop. (These are the soft green growths between two main leaves.)

Tender little seedlings make great food for birds. Keep them away by using either a crisscross of black string over the young plants, or just one straight black thread.

Plants which will be tall when they grow to maturity will sometimes need support. Put bamboo stakes beside them

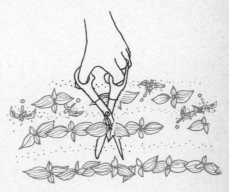

*To prevent root disturbance, thin seedlings by cutting them out at ground level.*

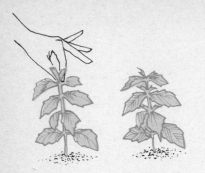

Pinching out the growing tips on many young annuals encourages bushiness and more blooms.

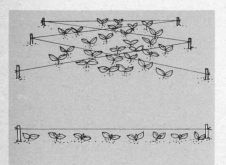

Black string will keep birds away from seedlings.

when they are still little so the roots will grow around them under the ground, and won't be violently disturbed later on. As the plants get bigger, fasten them loosely to the stakes with green string or wire twists. These will eventually be hidden. Snapdragons are a good example of this. If you don't stake the tall ones, they fall down and start to grow along the ground.

Once your annuals have grown up, they need three things to continue blooming successfully — water, food and pruning (sometimes called pinching).

## Water

Not all annuals need a great deal of water. In fact, some will be ruined   with too much moisture. These include impatiens, nasturtium, portulaca, and vinca. If you overwater these plants, you'll get spindly stems, a profusion of leaves, and few, if any, will result.

Some annuals, on the other hand, thrive in moist soil. It's important to check the individual requirements. The important thing is — don't overdo or underdo. For example, some people, in an effort to give their plants enough water, actually drown them. Too much water means that the soil gets drenched and can't bring oxygen to the roots. However, if the soil is allowed to dry out around flowers which don't like drought conditions, the plants can wither and die. Moderation and fulfilling the plant's individual needs will bring success.

## Fertilizer

Here is another instance of some plants like it — some plants don't. Everybody's favourite, the petunia, loves a good regular feed, as does the geranium. But with some annuals, fertilizing can stunt the growth of flowers and cause only leaves to develop.

Check the charts carefully to see if fertilizing is good for the plants you want to grow, and if it is, follow the package directions carefully. Usually one cup of diluted water-soluble fertilizer at the prescribed time is fine.

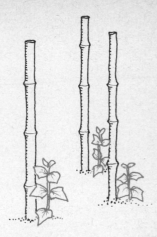

*Plants which will grow tall may need support. Put bamboo stakes beside them when they are young so the roots will grow around them and not be disturbed later.*

## Pruning and Pinching

Pruning primarily involves removing flowers. This can take the form of picking fresh flowers for arrangements. If you don't pick the flowers of snapdragons, for instance, they set seed pods and the development of other blooms is stalled or, in some cases, stopped. Be sure to cut as far down the stem as possible.

Dead-heading means picking the dead heads off the plants. It is important to pick or cut them right down the stem and not just

*As plants grow, loosely tie them to supports.*

*Dead-heading means taking the faded flowers off the plant. Make sure to pinch off right down the stem.*

*Pick the seed pods off plants like wax begonias so the strength will go into the flowers.*

pull them off at the top. Dead-heading encourages bushiness and further blooms, and prevents legginess — particularly in petunias.

You should also pick off any little flowers which may grow on foliage plants like coleus and Dusty Miller. Wax begonia, if it is planted in a shady area, sometimes develops green seed pods shaped like hearts. Pick these off as soon as they appear to force more strength into the flowers.

Remove any diseased or bug-infested flower immediately, and discard in the garbage — not on the compost pile.

If annuals such as petunias and lobelia start to look dragged out and leggy in the summer, cut them right back to the ground. They will grow back fresh and bushy, and continue to bloom until autumn.

## Diseases

Annuals are remarkably free of disease. Any problems which crop up can usually be dealt with quickly and easily.

Certain flowers, like the aster varieties, are subject to powdery mildew which shows up as white powdery spores on leaves and stems. This is a fungus disease and can be checked

If you see mottling and distorted growth on plants, especially asters, it probably indicates a virus disease. Don't fool around with this. Pull out the entire plant and discard it immediately in a plastic garbage bag.

Prevention is usually the best medicine. Earth which has been amended and aerated will help keep your annuals healthy, as will good garden practices. Always keep the ground raked clean and free of weeds and rubbish. Don't throw grass clippings and other material in a pile somewhere and leave it. Instead, dispose of waste material right away — putting discarded plants in the compost bin where it will do some good. Chop it up finely first.

Buy disease-resistant seeds and bedding plants. Sometimes seeds will have been treated with captan to prevent diseases right from the start. Don't soak the seeds or wash this fungicide off.

Water maturing annual flowers in the morning and at ground level to keep leaves and flowers as dry as possible.

## Insects and Pests
Most damage done to the leaves and young flowers of annuals is done by piercing and sucking insects.

### Aphids
Aphids are little brown or green insects that suck juices from stems and leaves, causing them to be stunted and curled.

They excrete honeyleavings which attract ants and harbour fungus diseases. Fortunately they are easy to get rid of. Spray the plants with an aerosol insecticide like Gardal® Rose and Flower Guard.

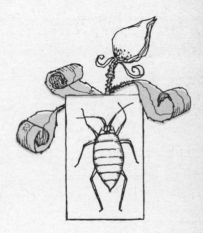

*Aphids*

## Flea Beetles

Flea beatles like young plants, and attack the tender shoot tips. This causes tattered leaves with small regularly-sized holes. Apply an insecticide like Sevin.®

Caterpillars

Flea Beetles

## Caterpillars

Caterpillars are a problem in the spring and summer, eating the edges of leaves and causing them to look tattered. Often you can pick the caterpillars off and dispose of them, but some are sneaky and just come out at night. In this case you should use insecticide like Sevin® or diazinon, or a systemic insecticide like Cygon® 240 E.

## Earwigs

Earwigs are little brownish beetles with pincer-like tails. They thrive in the underbrush, so good garden hygiene will help keep them down. Earwigs come out at night and chew through flowers and young plants ... leaving them tattered and full of holes. You can spray the affected plants with Sevin®, but the best method is to spray the earwigs themselves. Put a board down beside the plants and the bugs will congregate under it at night. The next morning, armed with a can of Creepy Crawly Spray®, turn the board over and cover the earwigs with a light spray.

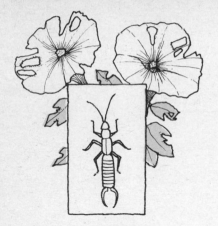

*Earwigs*

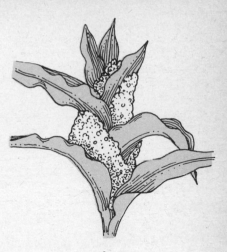

*Spittle Bugs*

## Organic Control

### Spittle Bugs

These attack young plants, causing deformities in growth. They are called Spittle Bugs because the they pile up on the plants looks like frothy spittle. Spray immediately with an insecticide like Sevin® or Banisect®.

If you don't want to use chemicals on bugs, dust the affected plants with Deritox™ Garden Guard® (Rotenone Organic Insecticide). Rotenone is made from the root of a South American plant called cube, and is completely natural. It kills bugs, but doesn't harm people or animals. The only drawback is, it comes in powder form and makes the plants look white until washed off. Still — it is completely non-toxic, safe and effective.

## Companion Planting

Another method of organic control is "companion planting".

Some plants can help keep the bugs away from other plants naturally. The ones I always put in my annual garden, and in my vegetable garden as well, are marigolds and nasturtiums.

Marigolds have roots which are toxic to many bugs, and the smell of some of the varieties keeps away other pests. They are good at repelling tomato horn-worms, nemetodes and leaf-hoppers. When you pull up the marigold plants, chop them fairly fine and put on the com-post heap. The resulting mulch around plants will act as a protectant.

Nasturtiums attract aphids to themselves, (where they do very little damage) and away from other plants which could be affected badly. They also repel other nasties like borers.

## Safety First

If you are spraying a small area, indoors or where there are no plants, an aerosol can of insecti-cide like Creepy Crawly Spray® might be just right. For a larger area and the use of a specific insecticide like Sevin®, you'll probably want to use a cannis-ter or a hose-end spray nozzle like Dial-A-Spray®. Mark any containers which have come into contact with herbicides with bold signs saying "Weeds Only" . . . then never use them to spray anything else.

Keep all garden sprays and insecticides high up, preferably in a locked cupboard, to protect children and pets.

*Keep fertilizers and insecticides off the ground and locked away to protect children and pets.*

# Chapter Six

**Annual Plants**

# Ageratum
### *(Ageratum houtoninum)*

| Condition | Solution |
|---|---|
| Light | Full sun or very partial shade. |
| Soil | Average to rich, well-draining. |
| Special Uses | Wonderful for rock gardens or containers. |
| Remarks | Over-fertilizing will encourage foliage at the expense of flowers. |

*Ageratum*

This low-growing plant, also known as the floss flower, originally comes from Mexico. Its compact powder-puff flowers make it one of the most popular annuals every year, providing a carpeted mass in borders and touches of feathery colour in rock gardens and containers. The most popular colour is blue, but you can also get verieties in pink, purple and white.

Seeds are slow to germinate, so it's a good idea to buy bedding plants from the nursery.

When the soil is warm to the touch and all danger of frost is past, dig a good amount of peat moss into the earth to encourage drainage. Then set out the plants about 6 inches apart and water thoroughly.

Ageratum is long blooming, and with proper attention remains attractive well into autumn. The plants grow to a height of 4 to 12 inches with a similar spread, but you can make them even bushier if you pinch out their growing tips early on. Water regularly, never letting the leaves get to the wilting stage, but don't over-fertilize — especially with a mixture high in nitrogen. This will result in too many leaves and not enough flowers. Feed once a months or in the middle of the summer with a low nitrogen fertilizer like Plant-Start® 5-15-5. Any dead flowers should be removed immediately, but further pinching back is unnecessary. Ageratum goes well with petunias, pinks (dianthus), and wax begonias. Try blue ageratum with orange or gold French marigolds for a dramatic colour combination at the front of the border.

## Alyssum, sweet
### (Lobelia Maritima)

| Condition | Solution |
| --- | --- |
| Light | Full sun. |
| Soil | Average to alkaline. |
| Special Uses | One of the best edging plants. Good for borders and ground covers. |
| Remarks | When first flowers have faded, shear plants right back for new growth. |

The delicate frangrance of this low-growing, spreading plant gave it the description "sweet". Irregular stalks, growing from 2 to 6 inches in height, bear intricate green leaves and clusters of small flowers in white, purple or pink. The plants grow quickly and bloom well past the first frost in the autumn.

Although you can buy bedding plants at the nursery an set them out about 12 inches apart, it is easier to sow the seed directly into the ground where the plants will grow. Sprinkle the seed into warm, raked earth, cover lightly with fine soil and tamp down gently. Water with a deft touch until the seedlings sprout, then keep watered regularly. The plants are fairly

Alyssum, sweet

hardy, but like a drink every once in a while.

Because it's so easy to grow (going from seed to full maturity in about 6 weeks), alyssum is an excellent plant for beginning gardeners, including children, as well as the more

43

experienced. Maintenance is easy. If the blooms start to fade in the middle of the summer, or the plants begin to look a bit scraggy, cut them right back and feed them with fertilizer like Super-Gro® 20-20-20. In no time at all you'll have a fresh second growth which will last well into the fall. As well as being a wonderful ground cover, alyssum is also good for awkward spots like driveway strips. Try planting it in hanging baskets as well. That way the fragrance can hit your nose immediately.

## Aster, China
### (Callistephus chinensis)

| Condition | Solution |
| --- | --- |
| Light | Full sun. |
| Soil | Moderately rich and well-draining. |
| Special Uses | Excellent for cutting. |
| Remarks | Rotate plantings each year to prevent wilt. |

Aster, china

The Western world was first introduced to asters in 1731 when a Jesuit missionary sent some seeds back from China to Paris. In the early 1900s the double aster was produced, and today there are over 200 different kinds available. As a result asters come in a fantastic variety of height, form and colour. They range from 10 inches for the Dwarf Queen Mix, to 30 inches for the Perfection Mix, in shades of white, rose, blue, pink and scarlet. The flowers can be ribboned, rayed, ribbed or curled, in varieties like pompom, peony and feathered. They all make excellent cutting flowers, especially the tall ones.

You can buy bedding plants,

but it's really best to sow seeds directly into soil amended with peat moss as soon as the earth is warm to the touch. Try to position the tall ones at the back of the border. They have a tendency to get leggy and look best surrounded by other flowers. Water regularly until seeds have sprouted.

Asters may need a little more care than some other annuals. They have always been susceptible to fusarium wilt, root rot and viruses, but modern strains have been developed which are disease-resistant. Look for these when buying seeds or plants. To help prevent wilt, buy seeds which have been treated with a fungicide like captan. Water plants from underneath so the leaves don't get wet, and sow in a new place every year. If you do find a sick plant in your garden, pull it out immediately and put it in a plastic garbage bag — not on the compost pile.

All this makes it sound as if asters are more trouble than they're worth but the opposite is true. Due to their infinite variety and outstanding cutting qualities, they are a constant in summer borders, and remain in the top ten of popular annuals.

## Baby's Breath
*(Gypsophila elegans)*

| Condition | Solution |
| --- | --- |
| Light | Full sun to very partial shade. |
| Soil | Alkaline and well-draining. |
| Special Uses | Gives other annuals a light, romantic look. Good picking flower for arrangements. |
| Remarks | Sow seeds every two weeks to ensure continued bloom. |

This graceful flower is known both as gypsophila and, descriptively, Baby's Breath. Delicate stalks growing to a height of 18 inches support masses of small star-shaped flowers, usually white but also red, pink and lavender. It not only softens up the look of a border, but is really wonderful as a picking flower since it fills out any arrangement beautifully, lasts a long time, and dries up instead of wilting. White Baby's Breath is

*Baby's Breath*

often used in bridal bouquets.

Root disturbance can disrupt growth and spread, so it's best to sow seeds directly into the area where the plants are to grow. Gypsophila likes soil which is alkaline and you may have to add lime if your garden is on the acid side. Start sowing the seed in drifts as soon as the earth is warm in the spring, then rake soil over and firm gently. Since the flowers will only bloom for a short period of time, it's a good idea to continue sowing the seeds every two weeks until the end of June or middle of July for a continuous summer display.

Once the seedlings start to grow, they need very little maintenance. Don't overwater or add fertilizer. The one problem is droop, but here's a way to solve it. Put chicken wire over the young plants and let the stems grow through the wiring. The plants will eventually cover the cages and the flowers will get the support they need without sacrificing the look of grace and airiness. As well as a border and picking flower. Baby's Breath can be planted between dry-set stones or around a patio.

## Balsam
### *(Impatiens Balsamina)*

| Condition | Solution |
| --- | --- |
| Light | Full sun or partial shade. |
| Soil | Moist, amended with organic material. |
| Special Uses | Attractive when massed in a small garden. Not suitable for cutting. |
| Remarks | Needs lots of water. |

This pretty plant has an erect single stem growing from 10 to 30 inches with flowers like tiny roses or camellias around it at intervals. Colours are white, pink, salmon and deep red. Balsam is also called Touch-Me-Not because when the formed seed pods are touched, they burst open emphatically. Originally coming from the tropical regions of India and China, it has adapted over the years to warm and even slightly cool summer weather, but still likes moist soil.

You can plant out seedlings about 10 inches apart, or sow seeds directly into warm, moist soil amended with peat moss. They will sprout quickly, usually within seven days. Once the seedings start to grow, feed once a month with a high nitrogen fertilizer like Super-Gro® 20-20-20, and give them plenty of water so that the leaves stay green. If insects start to chew on the plants, apply Cygon® 240 EC or other insecticide regularly. Make sure that the flowers can get the sun and are not being crowded by other plants.

*Balsam*

Pinch back some of the leaves on the stem if they are shading their own flowers.

Balsam was very popular in Victorian gardens and is enjoying a comeback today. The plants look delightful massed, or planted with low-growing, colourful annuals like impatiens (a not-too-distant cousin) and ageratum.

# Begonia, wax

*(Begonia semperflorens)*

| Condition | Solution |
|---|---|
| Light | Full sun or light to partial shade. |
| Soil | Well-cultivated with peat moss or compost. |
| Special Uses | Beautiful display when massed. |
| Remarks | Can be potted and brought indoors for the winter. |

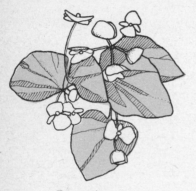

*Begonia, wax*

The wax begonia got its name because of its flat waxy leaves. These surround spreading mounds of delicate flowers, usually in shades of pink, but also white and red. For a while we didn't see too much of this garden staple, but its stunning appearance when massed and its easy-care nature have shot it back into popularity. Currently it is one of the top ten bedding plants in Canada.

In early spring, good young plants are available from the nursery and can be set out as soon as the soil is warm to the touch. dig in a substantial amount of peat moss or other organic material, then place the plants 12 inches apart to allow for spread. You can count on them growing equally high. Begonias like the sun, but also do well in partial shade although you may not get the same amount of bushy growth.

With a minimum of care, they will continue to bloom well into autumn. Water well, but let the earth dry out a bit between waterings, and feed about every three weeks with a double diluted solution of Super-Gro® 20-20-20 or other fertilizer. Dead blooms will just fall off by themselves, but if any green seed pods form you should pick them off so that the strength will go into the flowers. In the fall, you can pot the plants and bring them indoors for the winter.

Begonias look best when massed, and because they like

well-amended soil, they are wonderful in raised beds and containers. Try them as a border for taller plants, or with other low-growing flowers like ageratum.

# Browallia
### (Browallia speciosa)

| Condition | Solution |
|---|---|
| Light | Partial shade. |
| Soil | Moist and well-cultivated with peat moss. |
| Special Uses | Blue colour excellent in massings and in borders. |
| Remarks | Blooms should be pinched back to encourage side growth. |

Browallia, also called the Amethyst Flower, is a 12-inch-tall plant with graceful trumpet-shaped flowers, usually in shades of blue with a white eye, but also in pure white. It is a fine semi-shade plant, massed or in borders.

Browallia should be set into the garden as plants. You can grow the seedlings indoors or buy bedding plants from the nursery. Don't set them out too soon, however, as they like warm soil. Wait until the turned earth is really warm to the touch and the trees are in leaf, then fork in lots of peat moss and put the plants 10 inches apart. They grow well in partial shade, but an ideal location would give them the sun in the morning and shade in the afternoon. Eastern

*Browallia*

exposure is therefore ideal. When the plants are 4 inches high, pinch out the growing tips to increase side growth and bushiness.

Water frequently and feed every two weeks with a solution of Super-Gro® 20-20-20 or other fertilizer. Cut back in late summer and fertilize again for good new growth right up until frost. Then you can pot them and bring the plants inside for the winter in an area of bright but indirect light.

Browallia is also an excellent container plant, particularly with other semi-shade plants like impatiens.

## Calendula or Pot Marigold
### (Calendula officinalis)

| Condition | Solution |
|---|---|
| Light | Full sun or partial shade. |
| Soil | Lightly amended with peat moss but will tolerate poor soil if it drains well. |
| Special Uses | Good cutting flowers which can be dried. |
| Remarks | Use leaves in cooking. |

Calendula

Calendula or Pot Marigold can grow up to 2 feet high with single or double flowers in whites, golds and yellows. The flowers, 2 to 4 inches across, resemble daisies when they're single and marigolds when double ... hence their name. The word "pot" was added because the leaves were commonly cooked as a vegetable and used as a flavouring in stews. It has been grown for centuries and was a very popular plant in Europe and Britain during the Middle Ages.

Pot Marigolds like earth which has been slightly amended with peat moss, but also do well in poorer soil as long as it is well-draining. When the earth is warm, sow the seeds directly into the place where they are to grow. A second planting can be made in late summer for fall bloom as these plants are hardy enough to withstand light frost, and stay in flower until the beginning of winter. Full sun is best for this sowing, however.

To keep the plants bushy, pinch the growing tips out regularly, and cut back if they start to get a bit leggy. Calendula is subject to mildew so spray every once in a while with a fungicide like Funginex®. Water occasionally and early in the morning so that the leaves have a chance to dry off during the day.

Calendula make excellent cut flowers and can also be dried for use in arrangements if you tie the cut flowers together and hang them upside down in a cool dry place.

Try sowing Calendula in awkward spots like parking strips and side walkways for hardy growth and sunny colour.

# Canna Lily
## (Canna)

| Condition | Solution |
| --- | --- |
| Light | Full sun. |
| Soil | Rich soil with good drainage. |
| Special Uses | Tropical touch is spectacular by the pool or in patio containers. |
| Remarks | Rootstalk can be lifted and stored inside over the winter. |

This is a stunning tropical and subtropical plant which has adapted well to life in a warm summer as long as the soil is right. The leaves range in colour from green to bronze and look like banana leaves. The flowers, which resemble lilies, are held on long stalks and come in a variety of colours including whites, pinks, oranges and reds. The plants can grow to a height of 6 feet although there is a dwarf variety called "Phitzer Dwarf" which only reaches 3 feet and is good for containers.

The soil for the canna lily should be rich and well-draining, so amend it with finely composted humus —

*Canna Lily*

varieties come in the form of tuberous rootstalks which you can plant 5 inches deep and 10 inches apart as soon as the earth is warm in the spring. Be sure to choose an area where the plants will get maximum sunlight.

Spectacular in borders, canna is also a wonderful plant around the pool as long as the ground isn't too soggy. The flowers are best left where they are, but the colourful leaves can be cut and used in arrangements.

When the foliage begins to fade, dig the rootstalks up and store for the winter in a cool dry place — then plant again the following year.

from your own compost bin or from the nursery. Canna's many

## Carnation or Dianthus

*(Dianthus caryophyllus)*

| Condition | Solution |
|---|---|
| Light | Full sun. |
| Soil | Slightly alkaline, well draining. |
| Special Uses | Excellent for cutting and drying. |
| Remarks | Seeds can be started early indoors, or bedding plants from the nursery can be used. |

This is the border carnation which is smaller and bushier than the florist variety. The plants grow from 4 to 18 inches high, and the fragrant flowers, 2 to 3 inches across, come in white, pink, purple, red and salmon.

Carnations grow best in alkaline soil, so add lime until the Ph is 7.0. When the earth is warm, set out bedding plants about 10 inches apart and choose a spot which gets full sun. Pinch out terminal buds as they develop to encourage bushiness. The tall plants would be staked to prevent them from drooping.

Care is easy. Give them a drink occasionally but don't overwater. Since carnations are subject to rust, it's a good idea to spray them with zineb or Funginex®, about once a week. Keep pinching back to encourage side shoots.

Carnations make excellent cutting flowers, and also go nicely in borders and containers with other alkaline loving plants like Baby's Breath and

*Carnation*

cosmos. To dry for arrangements, hang cut flowers upside down in a cool dry place.

## Celosia or Cockscomb
### *(Celosia argentea)*

| Condition | Solution |
|---|---|
| Light | Full sun. |
| Soil | Fertile, well-cultivated earth. |
| Special Uses | Dramatic accent plants for border makes excellent dried plants. |
| Remarks | The showy flowers can be dried by picking at their peak, stripping off the leaves and hanging upside down in an airy place. |

Tall erect spires whose flowers resemble a rooster's comb. There are two basic types. The plume cockscomb has plumey flowers and some of them, called Chinese woolflower, have flowers like tangled wool. The crested cockscomb has velvety flower clusters. Colours are vivid — from yellows and golds

*Celosia*

striking accent right into autumn.

When the soil is warm, cultivate thoroughly until it is fine and then add sterilized manure. Bedding plants are readily available at the nursery. Choose young green seedlings and set out 6 to 10 inches apart. You can also sow seeds directly into the garden, cover with light amended soil, and keep moist until they sprout. Whichever way you plant celosia, make sure it's in a sunny location.

Water from beneath and feed once a month with plant food like Flower, Shrub & Vegetable Food 12-18-9.

to deep oranges and scarlets. Dwarf celosia grow from 3 to 10 inches while the taller varieties grow up to 30 inches and add a

Celosia are dramatic in the border — massed or with mums, marigold and zinnias.

## Coleus
*(Coleus blumei)*

| Condition | Solution |
| --- | --- |
| Light | Partial to full shade. |
| Soil | Enriched and loamy. |
| Special Uses | Luxuriant foliage provides contract in the garden. |
| Remarks | Can be brought inside to winter on the sill. |

Multi-coloured leaves, in variegated shades of purples, greens and yellows, are the main attraction of coleus. They are equally at home inside or outside and can grow up to 3 feet in the garden. Coleus grows well in soil which has been cultivated until it is crumbly, then mixed with lots of humus from your own compost bin or from the nursery. Choose a spot in the shade or filtered sunlight for best results, and set out bedding plants 12 inches apart. Once plants are established, you can propagate them from cuttings. It's fun and easy. Just break off a side shoot, take all but the tip leaves off, and place the stem in water. When the roots are 1/2 inch long, put the shoot in potting soil and keep watered.

*Coleus*

Coleus in the garden must also be kept well-watered to prevent drooping. Keep pinching back new shoot tips to encourage branching, and remove any little yellow flowers as soon as they appear. You should feed coleus every couple of weeks with a high nitrogen fertilizer like Super-Gro® 20-20-20, and spray occasionally with malathion to keep the aphids and mealybugs away. Coleus are attractive massed or combined with other plants in the border. In the fall, they can be dug up, potted and brought into the house for the winter where they will thrive in bright indirect light.

## Cosmos
### (Cosmos bipinnatus)

| Condition | Solution |
| --- | --- |
| Light | Full sun. |
| Soil | Average to alkaline and well-draining. |
| Special Uses | Excellent cut flowers. |
| Remarks | Flowers should always be put in water as soon as they are cut to prevent wilting. |

*Cosmos*

Average soil, slightly on the alkaline side, is just fine. Sow seed directly into the garden about 24 inches apart as soon as the earth is warm. Cosmos is good in many spots, as long as they're sunny, but is best at the back of the border where it can be supported by sturdier annuals. Even so, you should probably plant them in a fairly sheltered area well away from strong winds, and stake up the taller varieties at the base.

Care is easy. Don't overwater and don't fertilize at all or you'll get all leaves and no flowers.

As well as being a graceful addition to the garden, cosmos is a good flower for cutting. Be sure to put them in cool water right away or they will wilt.

Try planting in the border with snapdragons, Baby's Breath, and zinnias.

Cosmos is Greek for "beautiful thing" and this plant, with its airy gracefulness, lives up to its name. It can grow up to 3 feet high with delicate flowers like daisies on long wiry stems, and fine feathery foliage. The single-petaled flowers come in gold, red, white, pink, lavender and orange with tufted yellow centers.

## Dahlia, dwarf
### (Dahlia hybrids)

| Condition | Solution |
| --- | --- |
| Light | Full sun to partial shade. |
| Soil | Light, loose and fertile. |
| Special Uses | Excellent cut flowers. |
| Remarks | Tubers can be dug up and stored over the winter. |

Dahlias were brought from Mexico to Europe in the late 1700s and named after a Swedish botanist Dr. Dahl. Today there are well over 14,000 varieties available. Dwarf dahlias are bushy plants with attractive shiny leaves and single or double multi-petaled flowers in all colours except blue. The plants grow from 1 to 2 feet high with a similar spread, and the flowers are excellent for cutting. Dahlias are a good middle-of-the-border-plant — blooming from early summer right though to the first frost.

*Dahlia, dwarf*

The first year, set out seeds or bedding plants from the nursery 10 to 24 inches apart in very warm earth. Choose a spot which gets full or lightly filtered sun, and before planting, cultivate the soil with plenty of peat moss and sterilized manure. Keep pinching out the middle set of the three 3-leaved shoots as the plants grow to make them bushier.

Although dahlias like the sun, they also like cool roots, so keep a layer of peat moss or composted material around the base. Water well and feed regularly with phosphate and potash. Make sure you don't add fertilizer which has nitrogen in it, though, as this will weaken the stems and the tubers forming under the earth. Spray regularly with a fungicide/insecticide like Gardal® Rose and Evergreen Dust. Remove dead flowers immediately to encourage growth, and pick flowers right down the stem as often as you can.

After the foliage has been frost-killed, dig up the tubers and store over the winter in a plastic bag filled with damp peat moss in a cool dark place. Set these out again in the spring.

# Dianthus or Pinks
## (Dianthus chinensis)

| Condition | Solution |
|---|---|
| Light | Full sun or afternoon shade. |
| Soil | Moderately alkaline and fertile, well-draining. |
| Special Uses | A mild spicy fragance and frilly flowers add much to gardens and patio containers. |
| Remarks | Excellent cutting flower. |

*Dianthus or Pinks*

Dianthus has been cultivated for thousands of years and was Shakespeare's gillyflower. It got the name "pinks" not only from the colour, but because the indented edges of the flowers make it look as if they have been cut with a pair of pinking sheers. A relative of carnations and Sweet William, dianthus has single or double flowers in pink, white, red, and blue rising on wiry stems from clumps of attractive grey/green foliage. It can grow from 1 to 2 feet high with flowers about 1 inch across, lightly or deeply serrated.

As soon as the soil can be worked in the spring, sow the seeds right into the garden where they are to grow, about 12 inches apart. Add lime if the soil is acid, (pinks like a slightly alkaline soil with a Ph of 7.0) and amend with enough peat moss to make the earth well-draining. Pick a place in the garden which gets full sun or afternoon shade, and plant them in rock gardens and patio containers as well.

Care is easy. Water moderately and make sure water is draining off quickly. Snip faded blooms to promote further growth, but make sure you get the base of the blooms. Flowers at their peak should be taken out right down the stem as often

as possible since this also encourages growth.

Pinks love to be picked and
make an excellent cut flower in
arrangements. They have a light
spicy scent which is pleasant
but not obtrusive, and the variety of flowers and colours
makes them a pretty addition to
both house and garden.

# Dusty Miller
## (Senecio cineraria)

| Condition | Solution |
|---|---|
| Light | Full sun, partial shade |
| Soil | Average to sandy and well-draining. |
| Special Uses | Silver leaves make it a standout with vividly coloured annuals. |
| Remarks | Leave plants in the ground over the winter for even bushier growth the following year. |

Dusty Miller is a foliage plant
whose silver-dusted leaves are
the main attraction. People
notice and ask about it as soon
as they see it. It's a dramatic
addition to the garden — alone
or with brightly coloured annuals like geraniums and lobelia —
and it's reliable right into the
first snow. In fact, if you leave
the plants in the ground over the
winter, they will grow back
even bushier the following year.

Dusty Miller is particularly
good if you are planning a
garden you want to enjoy in the
evening, as it looks lovely at
dusk or in the moonlight. It can
grow up to 2 feet high if you
leave it over the winter, but the

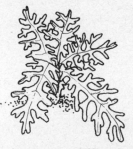

*Dusty Miller*

first year growth is usually
more moderate — 8 to 12 inches.

Buy bedding plants from the
nursery and set them out in the
spring as soon as the soil is
warm. Dusty Miller isn't fussy
about the soil it grows in as long
as it is well-draining. Add a bit
of peat moss when planting, and

place a full sun.

The growing plants don't need to be pampered, and can get along quite successfully with little or no fertilizer and moderate amounts of water. Every once in a while you can pinch out the little yellow flowers which might form, but that's about it.

What is sometimes overlooked is that this plant is outstanding for cutting. The leaves literally last for weeks with a minimum of attention and continue to look fresh. Just change the water occasionally.

# Gazania
*(Gazania rigens)*

| Condition | Solution |
|---|---|
| Light | Full sun. |
| Soil | Light and sandy, well-draining. |
| Special Uses | Outstanding massed or as a ground cover. |
| Remarks | Likes hot summers and tolerates drought. |

Gazania

Gazania is very attractive and easy to grow. Long sturdy stems support pretty and multi-petaled flowers resembling daisies, while fuzzy flat leaves hug the ground like a mat. These flowers love the sun so much that they close up on cloudy days or at night, and the colours are sunny too — cream, orange, yellow, bronze, pink and red. They will bloom right through the summer well past the first frost of autumn, and need very little care.

Gazania like sandy, well-draining soil and doesn't do too well in heavy clay or loamy earth. Set out bedding plants in a full sun location, or sow seeds directly into the place where they are to grow. Plant a lot of them in one place as they are delightful when massed or used as a ground cover.

Care is minimal. Don't fertilize at all, and only give them a moderate amount of moisture, letting the earth dry out between waterings.

Gazania does well in containers and rock gardens, and thrives in all sorts of odd places as long as they are sunny. Try planting the seeds between the dry-set stones in a walkway or patio, for example. They'll grow well in the sandy soil beneath. Then when autumn comes, you can pot up your favourite gazania and bring them indoors for the winter.

## Geranium

*(Pelargonium hortorum)*

| Condition | Solution |
|---|---|
| Light | Full sun. |
| Soil | Moderately fertile, well draining. |
| Special Uses | One of the most popular and successful container plants. |
| Remarks | Beautifully coloured plants can be wintered indoors. |

Geraniums are such a garden staple, they scarcely need any introduction. Sturdy stalks hold up clusters of small-petaled flowers surrounded by large lily-pad leaves. Red, pink and salmon are the most popular colours although the plants also come in orange and white. Sometimes the distinctive leaves are variegated with as many as four different colours. Usually treated as an annual, geraniums can be used again if brought indoors in winter. Just dig them up in the fall, pot them and place in a sunny window.

First time out, you should buy plants from the nursery. These come in various stages of growth, and the ones which have been growing for 2 or 3 years will naturally be larger and more expensive. Usually you can expect a first year geranium to grow up to 2 feet high with a similar spread. When choosing plants, look for

*Geranium*

Set geraniums out in soil well-mixed with peat moss. Since these plants perform best when their roots are constricted, they are wonderful in containers and actually bloom better that way. Geraniums are fond of acid, so every once in a while add some apple cider vinegar to the watering can. Fertilize every three weeks with Flower, Shrub and Vegetable Food 12-18-9. Whenever flowers fade, snip off right down the stem to encourage new blooms. They are attractive with Dusty Miller and lobelia. Try red geraniums with yellow marigolds for a richly dramatic effect.

hybrids which are disease resistant and heat tolerant.

## Grasses, ornamental

| Condition | Solution |
|---|---|
| Light | Full sun. |
| Soil | Average. |
| Special Uses | Excellent as a dried plant and as a striking accent in the garden. |
| Remarks | Can be sown into the garden. |

There are many varieties of grasses in colours of green, gold and purple. Most can be sown right into the ground where they are to grow, but the seedlings must be thinned out to about 12 inches apart. As they grow, they add a dramatic accent to the border. Water regularly from underneath, then cut and dry when the grasses reach their peak. Just pick before seed heads open and store in a dry well-ventilated place until grass is dry and ready to use. *Cloud Grass* — finely textured; white and pale green; 1 to 2 feet high. *Animated Oats* — 3 feet tall; hairy things on the flowers twist around with a change in the weather; self-sower so pick heads before they set seed.

*Quaking Grass* — 1 to 2 feet tall; seeds droop at the ends of the stems and "quake" with the mildest puff of wind; best massed.

*Job's Tears* — grown for its seeds which you can use to make jewellery; 3 to 4 feet high; soak seeds for 24 hours before planting.

*Hare's Tail Grass* — very popular; long-lasting flowers look like cotton-tails or hare's tails; best massed.

*Ornamental Corn* — 2 to 4 feet high; large striped leaves.

*Grasses, ornamental*

## Impatiens
*(Impatiens wallerana)*

| Condition | Solution |
|---|---|
| Light | Partial to full shade. |
| Soil | Light and crumbly, well-mixed with peat moss or compost. |
| Special Uses | One of the most popular and successful shade plants. |
| Remarks | Can be potted and brought indoors for the winter. |

Impatiens is the best shade annual around. The constant profusion of red, white, and pink single-petaled flowers over waxy green leaves make it one of the most popular annuals every year. It blooms through the summer until the first frost, with the Elfin series growing up to 12 inches high, and the Imp varieties twice as high as that.

Superior bedding plants are available from the nursery. Make sure you pick ones which

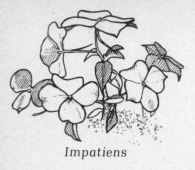

*Impatiens*

are compact, not leggy. As soon as the soil is warm in the spring, select a spot in full or partial shade and cultivate the earth until it is light and crumbly, adding lots of peat moss or composted material. Set the plants out the same distance apart as you expect them to grow in height.

Impatiens require very little care. Bugs, viruses, wilt, snails and funguses are generally not serious problems.

The only thing that might prevent the plants from growing well is improper watering and feeding. Because of their succulent stems, impatiens must never be overwatered. Although the earth should be fairly moist at all times, it should never be soggy. If the ground dries out and the plants begin to wilt, a good drink will revive them, but it's not a good idea to do this too often or the plants will get spindly. Don't add any fertilizer at all or you'll get all leaves and no flowers.

Impatiens is wonderful for problem shade areas under trees or on the north side of the house. You can also plant a twilight garden with white impatiens and blue lobelia or browallia.

## Lobelia
*(Lobelia erinus)*

| Condition | Solution |
|---|---|
| Light | Full sun or partial shade. |
| Soil | Average to fertile. |
| Special Uses | Good edging plant and outstanding in containers. |
| Remarks | Cut plants back in the middle of the summer for second growth. |

Lobelia is a lovely annual which deserves a spot in any garden or container. Small five-petaled flowers with delicate green leaves grow profusely from a single plant. Although it can sometimes be found in white, purple and even pink, deep blue is the most popular and outstanding colour. There are two types of lobelia — the bush or upright for borders, and the trailing for containers. The best upright variety is Crystal Palace which grows about 6 inches high, while Sapphire leads the way for trailing lobelia, growing 12 inches long.

Buy bedding plants from the nursery as seeds take a long time to germinate. Lobelia does well in all kinds of soil, but appreciates a bit of peat moss mixed into the earth in the planting hole. Full sun is fine as long as the summer isn't too hot and the plants get plenty of water, but lobelia looks fresher and more intensely coloured in filtered sunlight or partial shade. A spot receiving morning sun and afternoon shade is ideal.

Keep the soil moist but not

*Lobelia*

soggy, and try to soak it from underneath the plants so they don't get flattened. If they start to look scraggy in mid-summer, cut them back and fertilize with a solution of Garden Gro® B-16-12 Liquid Fertilizer for a fresh second growth.

Lobelia is a winner — by itself or with other annuals. The beautiful blue is stunning at dusk, particularly when it's planted with white lobelia, white impatiens, or Dusty Miller. In a sunny location, try it massed with yellow or gold French marigolds.

# Marigold, African
*(Tagetes erecta) and French (Tagetes patula)*

| Condition | Solution |
|---|---|
| Light | Full sun. |
| Soil | Average. |
| Special Uses | Pungent leaves of French marigold keep bugs away from other plants. |
| Remarks | With plenty of water, marigolds can survive very hot weather. |

*Marigold*

Marigolds, or tagetes, were originally sent back from Mexico by the priests accompanying Cortez on his conquests in the 1500s — first to Spain, then to monastery gardens in France and Morocco. By the time the flowers reached England, they were simply classified as French and African. Their orange and yellow colours earned them the nick-name Mary's Gold or marigold, and today they are consistently in the top five of popular annuals.

Both types like a sunny location with average soil mixed with a bit of peat moss, and bedding plants are readily available at the nursery. Buy them when they're round and compact, not leggy. French marigolds can also be sown as seeds directly into the place where they are to grow. African marigolds are the tallest, with the Climax and Jubilee series growing up to 3 feet. To help support them when they are large, set the young bedding plants about 3 to 4 inches into the earth, breaking off the bottom foliage and packing the earth around the resulting stem. Place them at least 2 feet apart. French marigolds will grow to 12 inches and should be planted 10 inches apart.

For bushiness on the taller plants, pinch out the axil growth between all the double leaves which form as the plants grow. Pinch any faded blooms off all types right down the stem. Give marigolds plenty of water from underneath and they'll bloom right through until frost.

# Morning Glory
## (Inpomea purpurea)

| Condition | Solution |
|---|---|
| Light | Full sun. |
| Soil | Average to poor. |
| Special Uses | Can provide a screen or cover. |
| Remarks | This vine can also act as a background for brightly coloured annuals. |

Morning Glory is the most popular annual vine. It got its name because the flowers would only bloom in the morning and then close shut in the afternoon and evening. Modern varieties, however, are being developed to stay open all day. The plants grow and twine up supports, forming a thick wall of single or double trumpet-shaped flowers with large heart-shaped leaves. The most widely grown colour is blue (with Heavenly Blue living up to its name), but the vine also comes in white, rose, crimson, and striped.

Plant seeds about 12 inches apart in average to poor soil with no ammendements. To speed germination time, you can either nick the pointed ends of the seeds, or put them in damp

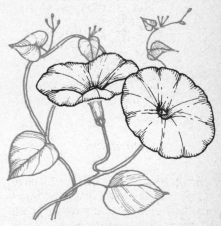

*Morning Glory*

paper towelling for two days before planting, and to help the flowers stay open longer, choose a spot that doesn't get too much direct morning sun. The growing plants will need some kind of support to cling to as they climb. You can make a trellis of wood, or use string, wire or rope — straight up and down, or as netting. Morning Glories can also be trained around unattractive objects like cement inset wells.

Keep the earth moist around the plants, but do not overwater or give them any fertilizer whatsoever, or you'll get all foliage and no flowers.

Morning Glories are lovely as a background for marigolds, petunias and zinnias, and can also be picked in various stages of bloom.

# Nasturtium
*(Tropaelum majus)*

| Condition | Solution |
| --- | --- |
| **Light** | Full sun. |
| **Soil** | Ordinary to poor. |
| **Special Uses** | Plant next to vegetables and climbing plants to repel borers and leafhoppers. |
| **Remarks** | Leaves can be picked and eaten in salads. |

*Nasturium*

Nasturiums are no-fuss flowers which are easy to grow and perfect for picking. An on-going profusion of single or double blooms grow up through largely lily pad leaves in clear oranges, reds and yellows. The fragrance is spicy but pleasing. The plants can be compact or climbing. The climbing variety is excellent for hanging baskets and containers, and can also be trained as vines if you help them by pushing the stems through wire fencing as they grow.

Nasturtiums thrive in poor

soil with very little water, and like a totally sunny location. Just push the seeds into the ground where the are to grow, after the first frost but before the soil warms up too much, as they germinate best in cool earth. If you want all the colours, buy different seed packets instead of the mixed seeds which usually turn out to be mostly yellow.

Don't overwater as this will produce large leaves and few flowers. Usually rainfall will provide all the moisture these drought-loving plants require. Never fertilize or add amendments to the soil or you probably won't get any flowers at all. The only persistent problem nasturtiums have is aphids, but a few good doses of insecticidal soap will get rid of them. Keep the flowers picked to encourage growth.

## Nicotiana or Oriental Tobacco
### (Nicotiana species)

| Condition | Solution |
| --- | --- |
| Light | Full sun or partial shade. |
| Soil | Enriched with organic material. |
| Special Uses | Especially fragrant in the cool of the evening. |
| Remarks | Attractive planted in clumps in large pots. |

Nicotiana has small trumpet-shaped flowers on long stems which bloom right into fall. The plants used to be famous for their sweet evening smell, although some of the newer varieties have lost this to a certain extent. The most fragrant varieties available are white N. alata gradiflora, or N. affinis. White is the most popular colour, but the flowers also come in red, crimson, lavender, and mauve. Growing up to 24 inches high, they look best massed or spaced between other annuals in the border as an accent.

Bedding plants can be bought at the nursery and set out 12 inches apart as soon as the earth is warm. Choose a spot which gets partial shade or filtered sun, although nicotiana will thrive in full sun if the climate is humid. Cultivate the soil until crumbly and mix in plenty of

Nicotiana

peat moss before planting. Don't put out anywhere near tomatoes. Nicotiana can contact tobacco mosaic virus, and while this won't hurt the flowers, it will make the tomates very sick indeed.

Nicotiana loves humidity, so be sure to keep their soil moist. Fertilize every couple of weeks with a solution of Liquid Garden Grow® 8-16-12, and keep the weeds down by mulching with peat moss.

These plants are also good in large containers and planters around the patio. The smell gets to you sooner, and you'll be able to watch the butterflies which nicotiana attracts.

## Pansy or Viola

(*Viola species*)

| Condition | Solution |
|-----------|----------|
| Light | Full sun. |
| Soil | Average but amended to hold moisture. |
| Special Uses | Lovely picking flower. |
| Remarks | New hybrids are increasingly heat tolerant. |

The pansy, from the French pensée meaning thought, is a very popular flower in the spring and early summer. Large five-petalised blooms in velvety colours look out at the world from longish slender stems, and are famous not only for their distinctive black markings or "faces", but for their fragance as well. Violas don't have the faces, but come in lovely muted shades of white, blue, mauve, purple and yellow. Both are hardier than they appear, and are excellent for city gardens and containers — growing successfully even in the midst of pollution and exhaust fumes. New varieties are being developed all the time which can also stand up to the heat of the summer.

*Pansy or Viola*

Pansies and violas are best set out as bedding plants at exactly the same depth in the ground as they were in the flat. They should never be allowed to dry out, so before planting, it's a good idea to amend the soil with peat moss or other material which will retain moisture. Then put a good layer of mulch around the plants to keep this moisture level constant and the roots cool. To help the plants bloom as long as possible, choose a spot which gets the morning sun.

The flowers will start to bloom immediately. Pick them regularly right down the stem, and pinch the plants back constantly to prevent them from getting leggy and to promote more blooms. Keep watered, and fertilize with Super-Gro® 20-20-20 every two weeks.

Indoors, pansies and violas look especially good in the uniquely designed containers which show the cut flowers to their best advantage.

# Petunia

*(Petunia hybrida)*

| Condition | Solution |
|-----------|----------|
| Light | Full sun. |
| Soil | Average, amended with peat moss. |
| Special Uses | Outstanding as a bedding and container plant. |
| Remarks | Good cut flower, should be picked to encourage blooms. |

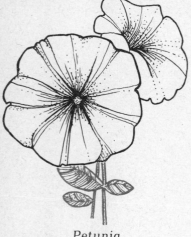

*Petunia*

Petunias, originally from Argentina, have become the most popular annual in North America. They are famous for their dependability and variety of colour — all shades of blue, red and purple, as well as white and yellow. The flowers, trumpet-shaped and about 5 inches across, come in single or double blooms — fringed, bordered or streaked — in compact or trailing varieties. The best trailing kind is Cascade, excellent in containers. Double bloom petunias are also good in containers as they have a tendency to droop over in the garden.

In the spring, as soon as the soil is warm to the touch, cultivate until crumbly and mix in some peat moss for good drainage. Buy bedding plants from the nursery — make sure they are compact, not leggy — and set into the earth about 12 inches apart. Pinch back to 6 inches. After the first bloom, cut back again. This will delay early blooming, but it's worth it in the long run as it produces bushier growth and more flowers.

Water regularly and fertilize at least every three weeks with Super-Gro® 20-20-20. Any faded blooms should be cut off right down the stem, not just pulled out of the bracket. Petunias make very good and long-lasting cut flowers with a pleasant spicy fragrance, and regular picking will encourage more blooms. However, if they do start to get leggy in mid-summer, cut them back ruthlessly, give them a good feeding, and in no time at all you'll have a spectacular second growth. With tender care, they'll bloom right into autumn.

## Portulaca or Rose Moss
*(Portulaca grandiflora)*

| Condition | Solution |
|---|---|
| Light | Full sun. |
| Soil | Average to sandy. |
| Special Uses | Grows in areas where other plants won't. |
| Remarks | May re-seed and come up the following year. |

Portulaca is often called Rose Moss. It is a happy flower which will grow in even the poorest soil as long as it's in the sun. A ground-hugging plant, usually only reaching a height of 6 inches, it has an abundance of single or double-petaled flowers rising above a thick carpet of succulent foliage. The colours — red, yellow, orange, white and coral — are clear and brilliant. The flowers love the sun so much, they just close up when it goes down.

*Portulaca*

Portulaca loves sandy soil in sunny locations so it is ideal around patios and between the stones of dry-laid walks. It is absolutely indispensible in trouble spots where other annuals just die out. So seed directly into the ground where they are to grow, but wait until the earth is good and warm and all danger of frost is past. Thin growing seedlings to 6 inches to promote bushy plants. You can also set out bedding plants 6 inches apart, as portulaca transplants well. Some varieties re-seed and come up the following year.

This is an easy maintenance plant, needing no fertilizer or grooming, and very little water. Rose Moss is not as well-known as some other annuals. Nevertheless, it deserves a place in beds, edgings and rock gardens, as well as troublesome areas like driveway strips. Try it with other ground covers like alyssum and vinca.

## Salvia or Scarlet Sage
### (Salvia splendens)

| Condition | Solution |
|---|---|
| Light | Sun or partial shade. |
| Soil | Fertile, well-draining. |
| Special Uses | Spikes provide a showy background for other annuals right into autumn. |
| Remarks | Grows from 1 to 3 feet so check for size you want. |

Salavia is a dramatic tall-speared plant which can grow from 1 to 3 feet. Although it is famous for its red colour, it also comes in white, lavender, rose and salmon — and in a blue variety which looks stunning massed or combined with the red. Salvia blooms all summer, thriving in the heat, but seems to come into its own in early fall with the colours of autumn.

Salvia can be set out as bedding plants as soon as the soil is warm. Amend the earth with peat moss or other organic material, and cultivate until crumbly. Plant about 12 inches apart. Scarlet Sage is a fiery, sun-loving plant, but it will also tolerate partial shade — making it a handy tall plant for tricky borders which don't get full sun.

Once a month, apply a double

diluted solution of Super-Gro®
20 20-20 to keep the leaves
green, but don't overfeed. Salvia
likes lots of moisture so water
frequently.

Because of the sweet nectar in
the flowers, a row of salvia will
sometimes attract bees, butterflies and hummingbirds. Try
planting the shorter varieties in
planters and containers with
white dahlias, and the tall red
ones in the border with the
golds and yellows of marigolds,
or the silver grey of Dusty
Miller.

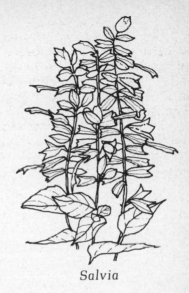

*Salvia*

## Snapdragon

*(Antirrhinum majus)*

| Condition | Solution |
| --- | --- |
| Light | Full sun or very partial shade. |
| Soil | Fertile, well-mixed with peat moss or compost. |
| Special Uses | Excellent for cutting. |
| Remarks | Flowers must be picked to prevent seeding. |

Snapdragons have spears with
individual flowers up and down
(which snap open when
squeezed) in clear lovely
colours — red, yellow, pink,
wine and white. The plants
grow from 6 inches to 36 inches
and come in three varieties —
dwarf, medium and tall. The tall
ones are good at the back of the
border, the medium-size in the
middle to blend with similarly
sized annuals, and the dwarf at
the front, or massed in their own
bed.

Set bedding plants out as

*Snapdragon*

6 to 12 inches apart, depending on the height. Pinch back as they grow to cause branching, and support the tall varieties with bamboo stakes.

You can fertilize in mid summer with Super-Gro® 20-20-20 but don't overdo it. Water moderately from underneath so the leaves don't get wet, as snaps are susceptible to rust. To be on the safe side, spray every once in a while with a fungicide like Funginex®. The single most important thing to remember if you want to keep your snap-dragons blooming all summer and into the fall is — keep them picked. If you don't, they will go to seed and the flowers will stop developing. Besides, snaps are so good in arrangements that they cry out to be picked. They also go very well in the border with other cutting flowers like asters, zinnias and marigolds.

soon as the soil is warm to the touch in a location which gets lots of sun. Turn earth with a garden fork until crumbly, amending with lots of peat moss or compost, then plant seedlings

## Sweet Pea
*(Lathyrus odoratus)*

| Condition | Solution |
| --- | --- |
| Light | Full sun or afternoon shade. |
| Soil | Well-cultivated with compost, slightly alkaline. |
| Special Uses | Wonderful for cutting. |
| Remarks | Vines can form a wall of flowers. |

Sweet peas have beautiful flowers growing up to 10 feet on tendril-bearing vines (or 1-2 feet on the bush varieties) in all colours except yellow. They like cool moist weather, but new strains can bloom throughout even a hot season with proper care. Their scent used to be exquisite, but has been bred out somewhat in favour of better flowers. However, the new hybrids being developed are trying to put the "sweet" back into sweet pea. Be sure to ask for these new varieties at your nursery.

*Sweet Pea*

You should set the seeds out first thing in the spring, so it's wise to prepare the bed the previous fall. Dig down 12 inches and crumble the soil up with lots of peat moss or compost, with a little lime thrown in to make the soil slightly alkaline. To prevent disease, change the location every year, but always try to choose a spot which gets the afternoon shade. When spring comes, sow the seeds as soon as the soil can be worked. Buy seeds which have been treated with a bacterial inoculant and Captan, and then just poke them into the already prepared soil. Provide support so vines will have something to cling to, and as they grow, pinch out any tendrils and sideshoots to produce strong main stems.

Fertilize every couple of weeks with a diluted dose of Flower, Shrub & Vegetable Food — 12-18-9, and water often. Place peat moss around the plants to keep this moisture level constant and the roots cool. Groom by removing any tendrils and spent blossoms as soon as they appear. The most important thing, though, is to keep the flowers picked — every day or two. They are so beautiful that this is no hardship.

# Sweet William
## *(Dianthus barbatus)*

| Condition | Solution |
|---|---|
| Light | Full sun to partial shade. |
| Soil | Richly composted and slightly alkaline. |
| Special Uses | Densely packed heads make it an ideal border plant. |
| Remarks | Winter in the ground for second year growth. |

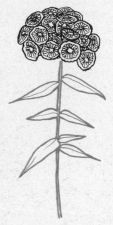

*Sweet William biennial*

Sweet William is a member of the dianthus family and a relative of carnations and pinks. It has thick stalks with green swordlike leaves beneath massed flowers heads. The sweet spicy fragrance is delightful, and the flowers come in wine and red with some varieties bi-coloured with white. The plants range in height from 4 inches all the way up to 24 inches so make sure you know that type you have before deciding where to put them in the garden.

Like its relatives, Sweet William prefers soil which is slightly alkaline. As soon as it is ready to be worked, fork it until crumbly, and add a generous amount of peat moss or compost. Dig in some lime as well to bring the Ph up to 7.0. Choose a spot which gets full sun or afternoon shade. Then, as soon as the soil is warm to the touch, set out bedding plants 8 inches to 12 inches apart — depending on height. Sweet Williams are hardy bienniels which will sometimes last through the winter in the garden, and bloom again the following spring. However, these biennials usually die out by the second summer and should be replaced by new plants.

Very little care and attention

is needed to maintain Sweet William, as it only requires moderate watering and no fertilizing at all.

Plant in the border with other alkaline loving plants — pinks, carnations and cosmos — as well as dramatically coloured salvia and snaps.

## Thunbergia or Black-Eyed Susan Vine
### (Thunbergia alata)

| Condition | Solution |
|---|---|
| Light | Full sun. |
| Soil | Average but well-draining. |
| Special Uses | Good cover for fences and trellises. |
| Remarks | Make sure support is in place before plants start to grow. |

Thunbergia is an excellent climbing vine which grows quickly to provide flowering cover. It has crisp leaves and bright flowers about 1 inch across in cream, orange and yellow, with black centres or "eyes" and purple throats. Since what climbs up can also cascade down, thunbergia is a popular plant for containers and hanging baskets as well.

The twining stems need support to climb, so make sure you have a wooden or wire trellis or other support before you plant. As soon as the soil is warm to the touch, fork it over and amend with peat moss to make it well-draining, then set out bedding plants 10 inches apart.

*Thunbergia*

Thunbergia likes lots of water, but you don't have to fertilize them unless they are in containers. Then you can give them a drink of diluted Super-Gro® 20-20-20 every month. Unlike the sweet pea, this vine doesn't have to be cut back or pruned in any way. Just let it grow. If you've planted thunbergia in containers, bring it indoors for the winter — container and all — then set outside again in the spring.

As well as being colourful and pretty, thunbergia can be used in a practical way to hide an unsightly spot in the garden or shade a patio.

## Vinca or Periwinkle

*(Vinca rosea)*

| Condition | Solution |
|---|---|
| Light | Full sun or partial shade. |
| Soil | Average but well-draining. |
| Special Uses | Hardy plant stands up to city living. |
| Remarks | Pinch back to encourage bushiness. |

Vinca is a pretty plant which blooms continuously all summer with very little upkeep. Small five-petaled flowers, surrounded by shiny green leaves, come in white, rose-pink, and white with red centres or pink with rose centres. It's very adaptable and is good as a bedding plant for borders, as a ground cover, or in hanging baskets and containers. It stands up very well to the stresses of city living, and actually thrives in hot humid summers. Although it is a

*Vinca*

spreading plant, rounded and bushy, it can grow over 12 inches high.

Vinca will do well in average soil, but you should add a little peat moss when planting to help drainage. Choose a spot in full or lightly filtered sun. Seeds are slow to germinate so it is best to buy bedding plants. Set them out 12 to 15 inches apart as soon as the soil is warm to the touch. Keep pinching out growing tips to encourage bushiness.

Care is easy, and simply consists of watering occasionally to keep the soil moist. Don't overwater, though, or the plants will get spindly, and don't fertilize. Plant vinca alone, or with zinnias, petunias or ageratum.

# Zinnia

*(Zinnia elegans)*

| Condition | Solution |
|---|---|
| Light | Full sun. |
| Soil | Well-cultivated with peat moss. |
| Special Uses | Wonderful cut flower. |
| Remarks | Keep picked to encourage blooms. |

*Zinnia*

Zinnias, with their brilliant daisy-like flowers in single or double blooms, are consistently in the top ten of popular annuals. They do particularly well in North America because of their fondness for long, hot summers. Zinnias come in a wide range of types and in all colours except blue, but they are most famous for the sunny colours of red, yellow, gold and bronze. The flowers are held on stiff stems with undistinguished foliaged. (It's a food idea to hide this in the border with other plants.) The different varieties can be divided into dwarf, intermediate and tall, and grow from 6 inches to 3 feet.

Zinnias are reliable and easy to grow. As soon as the ground can be worked, turn with a fork until it is crumbly and add plenty of peat moss or other compost. When the earth is warm to the touch, sow seeds 6 to 12 inches apart. You can also set out bedding plants, but be sure to buy ones which haven't started to flower or set bud. Choose a spot in full sun, and because zinnias are subject to mildew, plant them where the air circulation is good and breezy. As the young plants grow, pinch them back to promote bushiness and plenty of blooms.

Water frequently but carefully. To reduce risk of mildew, water early in the morning or at least five hours before the sun sets. Soak plants at ground level so the leaves don't get wet — one of the secrets of growing good zinnias is to keep the leaves dry. Spray occasionally with a fungicide like Funginex®, and fertilize every couple of weeks with a solution of Liquid Garden Gro™ 8-16-12.

Zinnias are excellent cut flowers and should be picked often to encourage blooms. Do this early in the morning when the buds are just starting to open, and the flowers will last a long time in arrangements.

| COMMON AND BOTANICAL NAMES | CHARACTERISTICS AND COLOUR | LIGHT AND SOIL | VARIETIES | SPECIAL USES | GOES WELL WITH |
|---|---|---|---|---|---|
| Ageratum or Floss Flower (Ageratum houstonianum) | Low growing feathery Plant, mostly in blue but also in pink, purple and white. Flowers look like pom-poms. Height 4" — 12" Span 6" — 9" | Full sun or half day shade. Average to rich well-drained soil. | "Blue Puffs" "Blue Blazer" "Blue Mink" "Summer Snow" (white) "Pinkie" (pink) | Wonder for edging, rock gardens or in containers | Dusty Miller petunias wax begonias yellow dwarf marigolds dianthus (pink or white) dwarf snapdragons dwarf zinnias. |
| Alyssum, sweet Lobularia maritima) | Low growing spreading plant, continuous blooming. white, purple and pink. Height 6" — 12" Span 12" | Full sun. Average to alkaline soil. | "New Carpet of Snow" (white) "Wonderland Purple (extra dark blue) "Wonderland Pink" (cerise rose) "Royal Carpet" (violet-purple) | Excellent ground cover, and one of the best edging plants. Good bulb cover. | Almost anything in full sun. As ground cover for tall, willowy annuals like cosmos and zinnia. Massed with lobelia, small marigolds, or petunias. |
| Aster, china (Callistephus chinensis) | Wide range in height and shapes. Petals often curled or quilled on (usually) double blooms. White, yellow, pink, White, yellow, pink, Height 6" — 30" Span 12" — 18" | Full sun, tolerates light shade. Moderately rich or sandy soil. | "Ball" rounded flowers with quilled petals. "Chrysanthemum" open and many-petaled. "Pompom" compact round flowers "Powderpuffs" double-flowered 2-foot-high. "Dwarf Queen" double-flowered 8" — 12" high | An outstanding flower for cutting. | Massed with other varieties of aster. Cosmos, snapdragons, petunias, zinnias. Alyssum as edging. |

| COMMON AND BOTANICAL NAMES | CHARACTERISTICS AND COLOUR | LIGHT AND SOIL | VARIETIES | SPECIAL USES | GOES WELL WITH |
|---|---|---|---|---|---|
| Baby's Breath (Gypsophila elegans) | Airy and graceful, with small white flowers on tall, delicate stalks. Also in pink and red. Height 15" — 18" Span 8" — 10" | Full sun, but tolerates some shade. Well-drained, alkaline soil. | Best white strain is "Covent Garden" "Rosa" (pink) "Carmen (red) | Delicate and airy in borders, lovely cut for bouquets and flower arrangements. | Cosmos, dianthus, carnation, snapdragon. |
| Balsam (Impatiens balsamina) | Upright plant with tiers of rose-like flowers. Lightly spreading. Red, purple, pink, salmon, white. Height 10" — 30" Span 8" — 12" | Full sun or partial shade. Moist soil. | | Good massed in small garden or in containers. | Petunias, impatiens alyssum, lobelia, ageratum. |
| Begonia, wax (Begonia semperflorens) | Spreading and low, with waxy leaves. Flowers are usually in shades of pink, but also come in white and red. Height 6" — 12" Span 6" — 12" | Full sun or partial to full shade. Well-drained, amended soil (peat moss or humus). | "Othello with bronzed leaves "Gladiator Red" large flowers "Pizza 33" series, bright, dwarf hybrids in mixed colours "Linda" deep pink | Lovely display when massed. Good in raised beds or window boxes. | Good massed with other begonias and edged with lobelia, alyssum, or ageratum. |
| Browallia (Browallia speciosa) | Small, trumpet-shaped flowers. Most popular is purple-blue, then white. Height 10" — 20" Span 10" | Tolerates full sun but is best in partial shade. Moist soil amended with peat moss. | Blue Bells" (blue) "Silver Bells" (white) "Sapphire" (compact blue) "Heavenly Bells" (deep blue) | Excellent semi-shade plant for borders and containers. | Impatiens, balsam, dahlia, dwarf Salvia, petite marigolds or massed together. |

| Name | Description | Growing Conditions | Varieties | Uses | Companions |
|---|---|---|---|---|---|
| Calendula or Pot Marigold (Calendula officinalis) | Single or double flowers about 4" across, look a bit like marigolds. White, ivory, gold, yelow, peach. Height 6" — 20" Span 6" — 12" | Full sun. Well-drained soil, lightly amended with peat moss. | "Golden Gem" "Pacific Beauty" (heat tolerant) "Orange Gem" "Suny Boy" "Flame" "Persimon" | Good cutting flower which dries well. Leaves can be cooked as vegetable. | Marigolds, lobelia, Dusty Miller, ageratum. |
| Canna Lily (canna) | Large green to orange leaves look like banana leaves. Tropical plant with flowers like lilies which bloom on long stalks. White, ivory, shades of yellow, orange, pink, apricot, coral, Salmon, and red. Height 3' — 6' Span 10" — 12" | Full sun. Rich soil with good drainage. | "President" (red flowers, green leaves) "King Humbert" yellow flowers, green leaves or red flowers, orange leaves) 'Phitzer Dwarf" (30" — 36" tall) | Good beside pools or in containers. Flowers are not good cut, but leaves are good in arrangements. | Best massed against plain background or green foliage. |
| Carnation (Dianthus caryophullus) | Smaller than the florist varieties but similar in appearance. White, pink, salmon, lavender, purple. Height 4" — 18" Span 6" — 10" | Full sun. Well-drained soil slightly alkaline. | "China Pink" "Princess" "Enfant de Nice" (red, rose, salmon, white) "Dwarf Fragance" (smaller but same colours) | Looks lovely in the garden and also makes an excellent cutting flower. | Baby's Breath, pinks, cosmos, sweet alyssum. |

| COMMON AND BOTANICAL NAMES | CHARACTERISTICS AND COLOUR | LIGHT AND SOIL | VARIETIES | SPECIAL USES | GOES WELL WITH |
|---|---|---|---|---|---|
| Celosia or Cockscomb<br><br>(Celosia argenta) | Tall spikes look like a rooster's comb. Red, yellow, orange, pink, purple.<br>Height 10" — 30"<br>Span 9" — 12" | Full sun. Fertile soil, amended with peat moss. | "Fiery Feather" (red)<br>"Golden Feather" (gold)<br>"Red Fox" (Carmine red)<br>"Apricot Brandy" (orange)<br>"Forest Fire" (fiery orange)<br>"Empress" (bright red) | Dramatic border plants in background. Good dried flowers, hold their true colours. | Phlox, marigolds, zinnias, nicotiana, ornamental grasses. |
| Coleus<br><br>(Coleus blumei) | Poor flowers, but great foliage. The leaves are borad and primarily variegated. Purples, greens, and yellows.<br>Height 8" — 36"<br>Span 8" — 12" | Partial shade. Light and crumbly soil. Needs lots of water. | "Carefree"<br>"Rainblow"<br>"Wizard"<br>"Fancy Free Mix" | Dramatic foliage provides contrast in garden or along driveway strips. Pinch back any little flowers and new leaves to encourage bushy foliage. Equally good indoors. | Celosia, oranamental grasses, border for evergreen hedge, Dusty Miller. |
| Cosmos<br><br>(Cosmos bipinnatus) | Tall, daisy-like flowers on wiry stems. Gold, red, white, pink, lavender, orange.<br>Height 18" — 48"<br>Span 18" — 24" | Full sun. Average soil. Do not overwater. | "Sunny Gold"<br>"Sensation"<br>"Radiance" (deep rose) | Good cutting flower and graceful in the garden. | Snapdragons, Baby's Breath, marigolds, alyssum, zinnias, asters. |
| Dahlia, dwarf<br><br>(Dahlia hybrids) | Low, bushy plants with neat single or double multi-petaled flowers. All colours except blue.<br>Height 12" — 24" | Full sun to partial shade. light, well-cultivated soil amended with organic matter | "Border Jewels"<br>"Early Bird"<br>"Red Skin"<br>"Annette"<br>"Irene Vander Swet" | Excellent plant for the middle of the border. | Lobelia, browallia, Dusty Miller, vinca, dwarf marigold, petunias. |

| Plant | Description | Conditions | Varieties | Uses | Companions |
|---|---|---|---|---|---|
| | Span 18" — 24" | (peat moss, or composted manure). | | | |
| Dusty Miller (Senecio cineraria) | Deeply cut leaves which spread and mound. Flowers are insignificant. Silvery grey foliage. Height 8" — 30" Span 12" — 36" | Full sun. Ordinary soil, well-drained. | "Siver Dust" "Diamond" | OUtstanding with brightly-coloured or massed annuals. | Geranium, lobelia, marigold, salvia, background for wax begonias. |
| Dianthus or Pink (Dianthus chinensis) | A relative of the carnation and Sweet William, this scented flower grows profusely singly or doubly on stiff stems. Pinks, whites, and reds, lavender, blue. Heigh 7" — 24" Span 7" — 24" | Full sun, tolerates a little shade. Well-drained, slightly alkaline soil, not too fertile. | "Baby Doll" (tricoloured white, pink, red) "China Doll" (semi-double, white with edgins in pink, rose, and red) "Magic Charms" serrated petals, white, pink, red) "White Lace" [feathery petals) | Good cut flower for miniature arrangements. | Baby's Breath, cosmos, carnations. |
| Gazania or Treasure Flower (Gazania rigens) | Long, sturdy stems support colourful daisy-like flowers which love the sun. Comes in sunny colours as well — yellows, golden-orange, orange, pink, red, and often in combinations of these colours. Height 6" — 15" Span 6" — 12" | Full sun. Sandy, well-drained soil, not too fertile. Needs lots of water. | "Mini Star "angerine" "Sunshine" | A real winner for borders, ground covers, containers, or rock gardens. Put between stones in the walkway. | Wonderful massed or as an edging for zinnias, salvia, snapdragons, and all kinds of marigolds. |

| COMMON AND BOTANICAL NAMES | CHARACTERISTICS AND COLOUR | LIGHT AND SOIL | VARIETIES | SPECIAL USES | GOES WELL WITH |
|---|---|---|---|---|---|
| Geranium (Pelargonium hortorum) | Pungent-smelling, multi-blossomed and hardy, on long stems. Also trailing varieties grown from cuttings. Red, pink, orange, salmon, white. Height 12" — 24" Span 12" — 20" | Full sun. Moderately fertile and well-drained soil. | "Show Girl" (pink) "Nittany Lion" (red) "Sprinter" (scarlet) | Outstanding in window boxes or containers. Can be brought indoors in the winter. | Lobelia, Dusty Miller, marigolds, ageratum. |
| Grasses, ornamental | Variously shaped sprays of grasses, no flowers. Greens, golds, purples. Height 12" — 18" Span 12" | Full sun. Average garden soil. | "Fountain Grass" (purple) "Animated Oats" "Cloud Grass" "Foxtail Millet" "Hare's Tail" "Job's Tears" | Can be sown directly into the back of the border. Good dried plant. | Goes with anything in a large border as a vertical accent. |
| Impatiens (Impatiens wallerana) | Excellent shade plant requiring little or no care. Single and double small flowers amid deep green, waxy leaves. Spreading. Reds, pinks, whites are most pupular. Elfin Height 6" — 12" Span 12" — 24" Imp Height 12" — 24" Span 12" — 24" | Partial to full shade. Light and crumbly soil mixed well with peat moss. Never needs fertilizer. | "Elfin" series "Imp" series "Blitz" has extra large blooms and tolerates some sun. | Excellent in shady areas around trees or on the north side of the house. | Good massed together, or with white lobelia or browallia. |

| Name | Conditions | Description | Varieties | Notes | Companions |
|---|---|---|---|---|---|
| Lobelia (Lobelia erinus) | Full sun or partial shade. Average soil. | Little flowers grow and spread among small green leaves. Most popular in blue, also comes in white and red. Upright and trailing varieties. Upright Height 4" — 6" Span 12" Trailing Height 12" Span 6" | "Crystal Palace" (dark blue) "Rosamond" (red with white center) "White Lady" (white) "Sapphire" (trailing, blue with white center) | Excellent plant for edging and one of the best for containers. Colours even more vivid at twilight. | Geraniums, impatients Dusty Miller, marigolds, petunias. Good massed in a solid colour or plant blue and white together for a stunning border. |
| Marigold, African Tagetes erecta) | Full sun. Average soil. | Large double flowers on tall, many-stalked plants. Most popular colours are gold, orange, and yellow, but white and cream also available. Bloom well into fall. Height 14" — 36" Span 12" — 24" | "Inca" series (orange, yellow) "Jubilee" series (yellow, orange) "Climax" series (orange, yellow) | One of the best back-of-the-border plants. | Mass with same type or others in species. Zinnias, salvia, calendula, cosmos, geranium. |
| Marigold, French (Tagetes patula) | Full sun. Average soil. | Smaller, double flowers on petite to small plants. Yellow, gold, mahogany, and variegated. Height 8" — 12" Span 10" — 15" | "Petite" series (orange and maroon) "Bay" series (orange, yellow, and bicoloured) "Solero" (maroon) "Red Cherry" (mahogany) | Marigolds make good neighbours as they repel tomato horn-worms, nematodes, and other pests including leaf-hoppers. | Lobelia, browallia, alyssum, dahlia, ageratum, geranium, pansy, viola. |

| COMMON AND BOTANICAL NAMES | CHARACTERISTICS AND COLOUR | LIGHT AND SOIL | VARIETIES | SPECIAL USES | GOES WELL WITH |
|---|---|---|---|---|---|
| Morning Glory (Ipomoea purperea and I. tricolour) | Strong-growing vine with single or double trumpet-shaped flowers. Needs support to climb. Blue is most popular, also in white, blue and white striped, rose, and crimson. Height 6' — 12' Span 8" — 12" | Full sun. Average to poor soil with not too much water. | "Heavenly Blue" (sky blue) "Pearly Gates" (white) "Flying Saucers" (white and blue striped) "Scarlet O'Hara" (crimson) | Can act as a screen for privacy or to hide unsightly view. | Massed for excellent show of flowers. Background for yellow marigolds, pink petunias, dahlias, zinnias, snap- dragons. |
| Nasturtiums (Tropacolum majus) | Graceful single or double flowers in jewel-like colours grow up between large round leaves. Also a climbing or trailing variety good for fences or containers. Yellow, gold, orange, red. Upright Span 6" — 12"  Trailing Height 2' — 3' Span 6" — 12" | Full sun. Average to poor soil without amendments or fertilizer and fairly dry. | Seed packets with mixed or separate colours. "Cherry Rose" (double) "Whirlybird" (single) "Jewel Mixture" (dwarf) "Gleam" (double) Hight 8" — 12" | Good picking flower. Helps protect vegetables and climbing plants from aphids and other insects. | Cosmos, dwarf marigolds, morning-glory, gazania. |
| Nicotiana or Oriental Tobacco | Small trumpet-shaped flowers, clustered on long stems. Plants bloom right into | Full sun or partial shade. Well-drained, fairly rich soil | "White Bedder" (white) "Idol" (dwarf deep red) | Smells very sweet, parti- cularly in the evening. Species "N. alata grandiflora" is the most dragon. | Dianthus, zinnia, cosmos, aster, celosia, snap- dragon. |

| Plant | Description | Soil/Light | Varieties | Uses / Companions |
|---|---|---|---|---|
| (Nicotiana species) | fall. White is popular, but also available in red, crimson, lavender, and mauve. Height 10" — 24" Span 10" — 24" | amended with organic material such as compost or manure. | "Crimson Bedder" (crimson) "Sensation" (assorted colours) | fragrant. Effective massed in a border. |
| Pansy or Viola (Viola species) | Large, 5-petaled flowers of pansies are held up on longish stems, and have black markings in the middle looking like tiger faces. Violas are smaller and do not have faces. Many colours in shades of white, blue purple, yellow, and red. Height 6" — 9" Span 9" — 12" | Full sun in spring, partial shade in summer. Average to rich soil which holds moisture. | Pansy: "Majestic" "Swiss Giant" (large flowers) Viola: "Blue Perfection" (medium blue) "Lutea Splendens" (yellow — a new strain available at nurseries which is adapted to cool springs and heat-tolerant for summer) | An excellent city plant; flowers ideal for cutting. Petunia, alyssum, ageratum, or massed in one bed. |
| Petunia (Petunia hybrida) | Compact or trailing plants are long-blooming with single or double flowers with some fragrance. Soft pastels to vivid colours — white, blues, and shades or pink and red are most popular. Height 10" — 15" Span 12" — 24" | Full sun. Average soil. | The main types are grandiflora, with large blooms, and multiflora with abundant flowers. Many varieties in both types. "Cascade" is a good trailing variety | Extremely popular for their colours and versatility. Can be used in borders, raised beds, and make an excellent container plant. Lobelia, Dusty Miller, geraniums, balsam. Wonderful massed with others in species. |

| COMMON AND BOTANICAL NAMES | CHARACTERISTICS AND COLOUR | LIGHT AND SOIL | VARIETIES | SPECIAL USES | GOES WELL WITH |
|---|---|---|---|---|---|
| Portulaca or Moss Rose (Portulaca grandiflora) | Single or double flowers on low, ground plant which only open up when the sun shines. Many colours including white, red, yellow, orange, and coral. Height 5" — 7" Span 6" — 24" | Full sun. Average to sandy soil, not too rich. | Many varieties in singles and doubles. | Colourful and sun-loving, this is a perfect plant for rock gardens. Also between paving stones and in the cracks of stone walls. | Ageratum, petunias, alyssum, vinca. |
| Salvia, or Scarlet Sage (Salvia splendens) | Tall spears are covered with a profusion of flowers set close together. Very dramatic when massed. The outstanding colour is red, but also comes in white, lavender, purple, red, and purple, red, and salmon. Height 10" — 36" Span 12" — 16" | Full sun or partial shade. Fertile soil enriched with organic material such as compost and peat moss. | Many varieties. "Carabiniere" (fiery red) "Red Hot Sally-New" (deep red) "Spendens Tall" (red, late flowering) "Victoria" (blue) | Long-blooming flowers provide a showy back-ground for other flowers right into fall. | Snapdragons, Dusty Miller, gazania, alyssum, browallia. Dramatic when massed with marigolds or white dahlias. |
| Snapdragons (Antirrhinum majus) | Spears are covered with closely set flowers which "snap" open when squeezed. Wide range of clear colours including white, pink, rose, and yellow. | Full sun, will tolerate a little shade. Fertile soil enriched with organic material such as compost and peat moss | Dwarf and tall varieties. (dwarf) "Little Darling" (semi-dwarf) "Coronette" (tall) "Rocket" (tall) | All varieties, dwarf to tall, are attractive in the garden and excellent for cutting. | Salvia, Baby's Breath, zinnias, marigolds, cosmos, asters. |

| Name | Description | Light / Soil | Varieties | Notes | Companions |
|---|---|---|---|---|---|
| | Dwarf<br>Height 6″ — 8″<br>Span 9″ — 12″<br><br>Tall<br>Height 20″ — 24″<br>Span 12″ — 36″ | | Many varieties of climbers. Dwarf non-climbers "Bijou" "Little Sweetheart" Intermediate climbers:<br>"Jet Set"<br>"Knee-Hi" | Best massed together with others of species. | |
| Sweet Pea<br><br>(Lathyrus odoratus) | A good climbing vine as well as a bushy ground plant. Equally fine as a cut flower. Lovely fragrance. Comes in virtually all pastel colours.<br><br>Climbers<br>Height 6′ — 12′<br>Span 6″ — 10″<br><br>Standard<br>Height 8″ — 30″<br>Span 8″ — 12″ | Full sun. Rich, organic soil, amended with compost, peat moss, and manure. | | Climbing vines form a wall of flowers. All types are fragrant, pretty, and good for cutting. | |
| Sweet William<br><br>(Dianthus barbata) | A relative of the carnation, this small to medium plant has densely packed single or double flowers over minimal foliage at the base of stalks. In shades of wine and red, some patterned, with good fragrance.<br>Height 4″ — 8″<br>Span 8″ — 10″ | Full sun. Average to fertile soil. | "Red Monarch" [red] "Roundabout" [patterned red] "Wee Willie" many shades of red | Hardy plants, often last right through winter in many parts of the country. | Salvia, snapdragons, carnations, pinks (dianthus). |

| COMMON AND BOTANICAL NAMES | CHARACTERISTICS AND COLOUR | LIGHT AND SOIL | VARIETIES | SPECIAL USES | GOES WELL WITH |
|---|---|---|---|---|---|
| Thunbergia or Black-Eyed Susan Vine<br><br>(Thunbergia alata) | An excellent climbing vine providing flowering cover very quickly.<br>Cream, orange, or yellow with a purple throat.<br>Height 6' — 10'<br>Span 6" — 10" | Full sun. Average soil, but well-drained. | Look for varieties of pure orange, orange with black throat, white with black throat, pure white, or mixed. | Good cover for fence or trellis. Excellent in hanging baskets. | Best massed as vine. |
| Vinca or Periwinkle<br><br>(Vinca rosea) | Low spreading plants with single 5-petaled flowers and shiny dark green foliage.<br>Pretty white with rosy centers, white and rose-pink.<br>Height 6" — 10"<br>Span 1' — 2' | Full sun or partial shade. Average to poor soil. | "Little Blanche" (white)<br>"Little Bright Eye" (white with rosy center)<br>"Little Linda" (deep orchid)<br>"Little Delicata" (pink with red center) | Very pretty plant is hardy enough to stand up to city living. Attractive massed as border. | Zinnia, marigolds, petunias. |
| Zinnia<br><br>(Zinnia elegans hybrids) | Single or double flowers with many petals in a wide range of plant sizes. Long blooming and reliable.<br>Many colours.<br>Height 6" — 18"<br>Span 6" — 18" | Full sun. Rich, well-drained soil. | "Thumbelina" (extra dwarf)<br>"Buttons" (semi-dwarf, double)<br>"Dasher" (semi-dwarf) | This is one of the best cutting flowers. | Effective surrounded with other plants like vinca, dwarf salvia, dwarf marigold, cosmos, snapdragons, and asters. |

# Cullen Garden Guides

A series of 8 garden guides written especially for Canadian garden conditions. Written by Mark Cullen, one of Canada's leading gardening experts, these handy guides are easy to read, yet packed full of the information you need for every situation. Titles in the series include:

**HOUSEPLANTS** by Mark Cullen   $5.95

**LAWNS AND LANDSCAPING** by Mark Cullen   $5.95

**WEEDS, PESTS AND DISEASES** by Mark Cullen   $5.95

**ANNUALS** by Mark Cullen   $5.95

**PERENNIALS AND ROSES** by Mark Cullen   $5.95

**PRUNING** by Mark Cullen $5.95

**CONTAINER GARDENING** by Mark Cullen   $5.95

If you can't find your favourite Cullen Garden Guide where you shop, you can obtain a copy by sending **$5.95** plus **50¢** postage for each book to:

Summerhill Press Ltd.
5 Clarence Square
Toronto, Ontario M5V 1H1

*Please allow three weeks for delivery*